Fundamentals of
Assurance for Lean Projects

An overview for auditors and project teams

Fundamentals of Assurance for Lean Projects

An overview for auditors and project teams

CHRISTOPHER WRIGHT

IT Governance Publishing

Every possible effort has been made to ensure that the information contained in this book is accurate at the time of going to press, and the publisher and the author cannot accept responsibility for any errors or omissions, however caused. Any opinions expressed in this book are those of the author, not the publisher. Websites identified are for reference only, not endorsement, and any website visits are at the reader's own risk. No responsibility for loss or damage occasioned to any person acting, or refraining from action, as a result of the material in this publication can be accepted by the publisher or the author.

Apart from any fair dealing for the purposes of research or private study, or criticism or review, as permitted under the Copyright, Designs and Patents Act 1988, this publication may only be reproduced, stored or transmitted, in any form, or by any means, with the prior permission in writing of the publisher or, in the case of reprographic reproduction, in accordance with the terms of licences issued by the Copyright Licensing Agency. Enquiries concerning reproduction outside those terms should be sent to the publisher at the following address:

IT Governance Publishing
IT Governance Limited
Unit 3, Clive Court
Bartholomew's Walk
Cambridgeshire Business Park
Ely
Cambridgeshire
CB7 4EA
United Kingdom
www.itgovernance.co.uk

The author has asserted the rights of the author under the Copyright, Designs and Patents Act, 1988, to be identified as the author of this work.

First published in the United Kingdom in 2017
by IT Governance Publishing.

ISBN 978-1-84928-898-9

FOREWORD

How do you measure the effectiveness of a Lean project? There are no standardised metrics, no predefined checklists, and no easy answers. Auditors and others performing assurance reviews of Lean projects need to rely on their powers of observation and their inquisitive natures to obtain the information that they need. Most importantly, they need to align their auditing methods to focus on assessing the three most critical outcomes of a Lean project: Increasing customer value, minimising waste and ensuring continuous improvement.

In the same way that Lean thinking changes the way in which people work, the auditing of Lean projects must change from traditional auditing approaches to methods that are more customer-centric, more focused on identifying areas of waste, and better able to monitor ongoing improvement. Lean audits do not negate the importance of confirming efficiencies, adequate controls and effective governance; they do, however, revolutionise the way in which these core objectives are gathered, assessed and documented. The challenge is finding the right tools to help you make the transition from traditional auditing to Lean audits.

Fundamentals of Assurance for Lean Projects is a practical guide that gives you the critical information that you need to conduct successful Lean audits across every business sector. This book is filled with practical questions that auditors can ask to address the key Lean objectives of minimising waste, increasing customer value and ensuring continuous improvement. It includes a refreshing number of real life examples that detail the benefits of conducting reviews of Lean projects and identifies the risks of trying to apply traditional auditing methods to Lean organisations. I am confident that every reader will walk away with a powerful set of tools that they can use in all of their future work.

Jamie Lynn Cooke, CSM, CSPO

Author of award-winning books on Agile methods, including *Agile Productivity Unleashed: Proven approaches for achieving real productivity gains in any organization.*

PREFACE

Lean and agile. Phrases not usually used to describe auditors and other risk management specialists! But increasingly we are asked to provide advice and assurance on agile and lean projects. As their names imply, these projects require fast, low cost and low impact reviews – whilst still providing stakeholders with useful assurance and advice. Since I wrote my first book on agile audit (*Agile Audit and Governance*), an increasing number of clients and contacts have been asking me about lean. Although this approach is still rare for pure IT projects where Agile Scrum still dominates, it is becoming very common as the basis for business based change and transformation projects, and we are also seeing a spread of 'lean start-ups'. There are new risks associated with these projects including:

- Is the project cost effective?
- Will it achieve its objectives?
- What are the impacts of the project on other parts of the business?
- How about project management, governance and compliance?

Management are keen to ensure that governance and compliance are in place, but without proper guidance the assurer could provide inappropriate advice – leading to delays and costs. The most common reason for this is a lack of understanding by the reviewer. As a result, they seek to apply tools and techniques they are comfortable with – rather than providing valuable input. This can be wasteful of time and effort which is not in line with the lean philosophy. Also, conclusions and recommendations can be flawed. Hence the need for this book.

I remember in the mid 1970s my father needed to buy a specialised four wheel drive light truck. I went with him on some of the fact finding. It came down to two potential truck makers:

Supplier 1 – UK based and very local to us, had many vehicles in stock but none to meet the requirements. They could produce one in six months but it would still then need to go to a coachbuilder for further refinements to meet the specification. We visited the factory production line and saw demotivated staff working on trivial tasks. We knew that this producer had problems with quality.

Supplier 2 – Japanese based, could deliver to the full specification in three months, even if it required some of the modifications to be made on the ship as the vehicle was transported to the UK. The supplier had a reputation for high quality and price was negotiable.

This was probably the first time I had encountered the lean phenomena and may illustrate one of the reasons for the demise of the UK owned mass vehicle producers. By the way, he had to choose the local option – which proved to be the wrong choice!

My very first audit in internal audit, over 35 years ago, was to help with a management/operational review of the leisure and recreation facilities at Leicester City Council. Instead of the normal focus on cash controls, etc. we looked at the processes for room booking, cash receipting, staff planning and management. We were concerned to ensure that these processes had minimal waste and were fit for purpose. They needed to provide good value for money, based on what would become known as the '3 Es':

Economy – were the required resources provided at an appropriate cost?

Efficiency – were these applied in a cost effective way to produce useful outputs with minimal costs?

Effectiveness – were the theatres and centres doing the right things? Were their objectives in line with what customers actually needed and wanted (e.g. opening times for swimming pools, etc.)?

Today, if we used similar techniques it would be classed as a 'lean' review, as it aimed to improve quality and customer satisfaction whilst reducing costs. Over the years I have conducted a number of these reviews including hospital pharmacy and pathology labs, IT service provision, local authority planning, housing and property repairs. I have also provided assurance for agile and lean projects, providing turnaround solutions where possible, and recommending the abandonment of the project where final costs would not have provided adequate payback from the benefits likely to be achieved.

I have written this book to share this knowledge and experience with you, the reader. My aim is to smash through some of the jargon and mystique that surrounds lean and provide you with some guidance and tips on how to perform audits, or assurance reviews, for these projects. When undertaking an assurance review of lean projects, many of the governance and audit principles for other projects still need to be considered (control of time, costs, quality and production of stated business benefits).

Finally, I believe that when conducting audits we should 'practise what we preach' and so should use lean tools and techniques in the actual conduct of our reviews – I have included a chapter on this at the end of the book. As with all books in the 'Fundamentals' series, it provides an introduction to the subject and includes references for those who would like to further investigate specific areas.

ABOUT THE AUTHOR

A qualified accountant, Certified Information Systems Auditor and Certified ScrumMaster™, Chris has over 35 years' experience of providing project and IT advisory and risk management services. He worked for 16 years at KPMG where he managed a number of major IS audit and risk assignments, including reviews of project risks and business controls. He was head of information risk training in the UK and also ran training courses overseas, including India and throughout mainland Europe. He has worked in a wide range of industry sectors, including oil and gas, public sector, aviation and travel. These assignments have included the review of value for money and cost reduction projects, including lean projects.

For the past nine years he has been an independent consultant specialising in financial, SOX and operational controls for major ERP implementations, mainly at oil and gas enterprises.

He is an international speaker and trainer on agile audit and governance issues, and has published three other titles for ITGP:

1. *Agile Governance and Audit* (2014)
2. *Reviewing IT in Due Diligence* (2015)
3. *Fundamentals of Information Risk Management Auditing* (2016).

ACKNOWLEDGEMENTS

Writing is as much about learning as communicating – and I have learnt a tremendous amount whilst writing this book. There is so much good stuff out there and I have found the Web particularly helpful during my research. Every book on lean thinking should acknowledge the great thought leadership on the subject from James P Womack, etc. and also from the Japanese pioneers who took a risk which paid off! I would also like to thank all of my former colleagues, and those who have attended my training sessions, for their suggestions and support.

I also greatly appreciate the support and advice provided by my friends and former colleagues in the production of this book. In particular, the support, and of course, the patience and guidance of my wife, Amanda.

As always, I have received great patience and support from the publisher, ITGP, particularly from Vicki Utting and Sophie Sayer. Also many thanks to their reviewers, James C Paterson, Jamie Lynn Cooke and Maarten Souw, for their valuable advice and guidance.

CONTENTS

Contents

Contents

Contents

CHAPTER 1: INTRODUCTION TO THE HISTORY AND NATURE OF LEAN PROJECTS

Overview

Before we consider lean thinking/projects it is useful to clarify a definition, look at the history, and consider some of the variants of how it is used today. This is useful, as many organisations use the phrase 'lean' to merely mean cost cutting, without any real understanding of the approach or how it should be applied. These factors will be the main consideration of this chapter.

Lean – A definition

We could define lean thinking as:

> Improving processes to ensure **maximum customer value** whilst **minimising waste** through **continuous improvement**.

Simple – and not a single Japanese word (more of that later)! Although there are many, and varied, definitions for lean manufacturing/thinking projects, they all generally focus on the same three key elements of customer value, minimising waste and continuous improvement.

The first part of the definition relates to 'customer value'. Free markets should be based on what customer's demand – a simple supply and demand model, unlike command economies where customers are 'given what they get'. Most organisations claim they are delivering their customer's needs. In some cases, however, this is not due to the pull effect, based on customer demands and preferences, that one would expect. There is still a push element, where suppliers are restricting which markets they operate in and how they offer their product – especially if they operate in an area of low competition.

The second component of the definition, 'minimising waste', helps to reduce cost so products can be sold at a competitive price, whilst still allowing a profit margin for the maker/provider and those involved in the supply chain to get the goods or services to the customer. Waste can come in many forms – we will consider these later in the book, based on the three Japanese terms:

1. 'Muda' (futility/uselessness) – e.g. doing actions that provide little or no benefit
2. 'Mura' (unevenness) – e.g. unnecessary downtime
3. 'Muri' (unreasonable/impossible) – e.g. unreasonable workloads or failure to effectively use the skill sets of staff available.

The third part of the definition is continuous improvement – constantly trying to improve the delivery of customer value and reduction of waste. This is true of the lean approach itself, where new thinking and tools are regularly being added to the publicly available lexicon of lean knowledge. As technology, fashions, working arrangements and economic conditions change, organisations need to also adapt and change.

So, the above definition of lean has nothing to do with its alternative dictionary meaning of slanting or 'deviating from the perpendicular' – although this could be a valid definition for some of the projects I have been asked to review that were no longer of value to the organisation!

The basic principles of lean should be intrinsic to all businesses – I have never come across a business that has a mission statement:

'To carry on making products that no-one wants to buy, using maximum effort and creating loads of stuff we throw away – even though this has never worked for us in the past, we refuse to change!'

Lean is not a project methodology – it is more a way of thinking and considering a 'process' or series of steps, to achieve stated goals. In this case, maximising the value to customers whilst minimising waste. The lean 'model' is hence a mindset based on a group of practices, strategies, tools and methods that can be applied to help organisations achieve these objectives, whether they are in manufacturing, the service sector, or the public sector, such as the NHS. In all these cases, where lean has been successful it is because it has brought about a long-term evolution change of culture, to focus on the three fundamental areas (waste, customer value and continuous improvement).

We will explore the fundamental concepts of lean in the later chapters, including the challenges that we face as auditors and reviewers of lean initiatives and projects. Whilst much of this is based on the manufacturing sector, the principles, tools and techniques can be applied to any project, including software development and organisational change.

1: Introduction to the History and Nature of
Lean Projects

It is useful to first consider the history of lean and some of the variation and other approaches which overlap with lean (e.g. six sigma and agile).

History

If I want to provide a service or product there are three main ways I can do this:

1. Provide a highly tailored craft based solution to meet the specific requirements of every customer.
2. Provide a standard mass produced product.
3. Provide a lean based manufactured product.

The attributes of each of these are compared and contrasted in *Table 1*.

**Table 1: Comparison of craft, mass and lean
manufacturing**

Craft	Mass	Lean
Low volume/higher cost	High volume/lower cost	Can be either
Distributed but may require parts from many locations	Single site	Distributed but co-ordinated
Aim is perfection	Aim is generally good enough	Aim is perfection
Customer gets specific requirement	Customer gets what we supply	We tailor what we supply when it is reasonable to do so

Craft	Mass	Lean
Requires high-level skill and training	De-skilled where possible	Requires some skill, teamwork, etc. as important
Produce by specific order	Produce into store	Production based on anticipated levels of demand (JIT)
Car manufacturing examples, Morgan and Rolls Royce	Big name UK and US manufacturers, up to about 2000	Initially Japanese manufacturers, now spread to others

Each still has its merits, however, there has generally been revolutionary and evolutionary movement from craft to lean via mass production. There are three main events usually connected with the history of lean manufacturing:

1. Henry Ford and factory production
2. Kiichiro Toyoda and Taiichi Ohno in the 1930s
3. Most sources date the advent of lean thinking back to Womack and Jones' publication *Lean Thinking* from 1996 and *The Machine that Changed the World.*

Ford is often cited as an early adopter of lean manufacturing because of his development of the automobile production line. There are earlier cases, however, where some of the elements can be found – for example, the Venice Arsenal of the 1450s and the Lancashire cotton mills of the 18th and 19th centuries. Many of these mills were designed around the locality of power – either water or coal for steam – and the process flow was from the reception of raw cotton through to the despatch of finished cloth – with various processes for cleaning, spinning and weaving in between. Given the relative cheapness of materials, labour – and indeed lives – there was little need for emphasis on cost reduction other than the profit motivation of the mill owners.

Ford did make some interesting changes to factory production, including:

- Use of standardisation of interchangeable parts – prior to this most cars were hand built for individual customers and so could not be mass produced.
- Introduction of flow production in the form of a moving assembly line, with operators assigned to specific sub tasks, aligned where possible in a sequence.
- BUT … Restriction of customer choice (not lean) – 'Any colour as long as it's black'!

The implementation of more complex machinery and demand for variety in the car industry, led ultimately to a more modern approach being developed by Kiichiro Toyoda and Taiichi Ohno at Toyota. The focus changed from individual sub-processes to the flow through the overall process, with an emphasis on quality and monitoring. The aim was to provide what customers wanted at a low cost. Womack, Roos and Jones then codified this into the five lean principles:

1. Identify Customers and Specify **Value**
2. Identify and Map the **Value Stream**
3. Create **Flow** by Eliminating Waste
4. Respond to Customer **Pull**
5. Pursue **Perfection**.

We will consider these in more detail in the next and subsequent chapters.

Although lean started in manufacturing, the principles have been used in several other areas, including:

- NHS improvement programme
- software development and change (*see Chapter 9*)
- management and audit review (*see Chapter 10*)
- start-up of new businesses
- business change, finance and HR.

Lean start-up – build/measure/learn

The publication, *The Lean Startup* by Eric Ries, provides a methodology to establish and develop businesses using lean thinking. It involves the lean concepts of building, measuring and learning, creating a product, and innovative high-risk experimentation. The emphasis is on getting a product to market as quickly as possible (the 'MVP' or 'Minimum Viable Product' and then developing it further).

There are five principles for lean start-up:

1. Entrepreneurs are everywhere
2. Entrepreneurship is management
3. Validated learning
4. Build-Measure-Learn
5. Innovation accounting.

The principles are based on lean thinking – the difference is how they are applied. The intention was to provide a basis for entrepreneurs to quickly get a product out, in a way that will reveal any failures quickly, so they can be resolved. In effect, getting customers to do some of the testing. Although this may be against our natural risk avoidance as auditors, if properly handled, it can be very beneficial. For example, by releasing the product to trusted customers who many feel honoured to try out the features before general release. At our local Nepalese restaurant we are VIP customers and the proprietor will often ask us to try new meals or drinks before they are put onto the menu.

The same principles can be applied to the start-up of any new product or project within an existing organisation. There is even mention of this approach in the *PRINCE2®️ Agile Guide* from Axelos.

Where does lean fit with agile and kanban?

Agile is a series of approaches used in managing software development and similar projects. The accepted definition is as per the Agile Manifesto:

'We are uncovering better ways of developing [products] by doing it and helping others do it. Through this work we have come to value:

- **Individuals and interactions** over **processes and tools**
- **Working [products]** over **comprehensive documentation**
- **Customer collaboration** over **contract negotiations**

- **Responding to change** over **following a plan**

    That is while there is value in the items on the right, we value the items on the **left** more.'[1]

There are obvious similarities to lean, as agile itself could be considered as a lean approach being lean, light, adaptable and flexible. Indeed, the two approaches can be used alongside each other. Another way of considering the two approaches is:

- lean thinking provides the what (requirements)
- agile thinking provides the how (implementation).

Kanban is an approach often used alongside lean. Kanban is a Japanese word with two meanings:

1. Sign or 'large visual board' (as written in Chinese characters – 'looking at the board')
2. Signal cards (as written in the Japanese alphabet).

Kanban has come to mean a methodology for lean and 'just in time' manufacturing (and other processes), to synchronise the rate of production with the rate of demand.

Key features are:

- A pull philosophy of customised production rather than the traditional push of mass production.
- Limiting work in progress (e.g. 'stop starting and start finishing').
- The use of a kanban lens.

---

[1] Source: Martin Fowler & Jim Highsmith. The Agile Manifesto. Software development, 8 August 2001.

The approach is based on four values and six practices.

The four values, or foundational principles, are:

1. Start with what you do now
2. Agree to pursue evolutionary change
3. Initially respect existing roles, etc.
4. Encourage leadership acts at all levels.

The six general practices are:

1. Visualise (with a kanban)
2. Limit work in progress
3. Manage flow
4. Make policies explicit
5. Implement feedback loops
6. Improve collaboratively and evolve through experimentation.

We will consider how kanban is used in lean in *Chapter 6*.

Lean six sigma (aka six sigma lean)

Lean six sigma seeks to combine the speed of the lean thinking with the quality of the six sigma approach. Six sigma has a number of tools, processes and even qualifications (in the form of 'belts') that can be applied in a lean environment. The concepts were first published by Michael George and Robert Lawrence Jr in 2002 in *Lean Six Sigma: Combining Six Sigma Quality with Lean Speed*.

Lean six sigma uses the DMAIC model from six sigma:

Define	Scoping the problem to be fixed, including high-level definition and agreement of scope with the organisation's leadership.
Measure	Obtaining a baseline of current performance, by data collection and enabling root cause analysis.
Analyse	Review the data obtained from measurements to narrow down root cause of defects and other waste. May require additional measurement to be performed.
Improve	Identify how the problem will be fixed, develop a solution based on innovation.
Control	Seek to transfer the improvements to 'Business As Usual' (BAU) and embed within normal processes and activities.

Lean projects

Lean thinking is also applied in projects – particularly for software development or business change, including changes to sales, launching of new projects, and business re-organisations or mergers and acquisitions. We will see later in the book that such projects may involve large or incremental changes. In all of these cases the same principles of customer focus, cost reduction and continuous improvement still apply. Hence I have not differentiated between 'lean thinking' and 'lean projects' in the text. *Chapters 8* and *9* will, however, also focus on some of the specifics relating to projects.

Audit considerations

An auditor, or other reviewer, should consider the extent of how lean is being applied for the organisation being reviewed. This top level approach will help to ensure that lessons learnt are applied throughout the organisation and that maximum benefit is being obtained from the lean activity. The following questions will help prepare an audit or assurance review to clarify this, by looking at customer value, minimising waste and seeking continuous improvement.

Auditors should never be afraid of asking dumb questions – they often generate some interesting and unexpected answers. When first investigating a project for review its useful to get some good contextual background knowledge.

Customer value

- How have you identified the current and potential customers for the product/service?
- How have you sought their opinions on what should be provided and what is the most important aspect to them? What do they need/want/desire?
- Are there any other stakeholders who need to be considered?
  o Customer proxies (e.g. regulators, such as Ofwat, Ofgem, FCA, etc.)
  o Shareholders and potential investors
  o The Board.

Minimise waste

- How are you identifying, categorising and assessing potential waste?
- How are you ensuring that this project does not lead to wasteful activity elsewhere?

Continuous improvement

- How will you ensure that the output from the project evolves to keep up to date with internal and external changes?
- How will you monitor post implementation to identify any small changes that can be made to further improve customer value or reduce waste?

Summary

In this chapter we have introduced the lean approach and principles, with the emphasis on customer value, waste reduction and continuous improvement, and considered how it fits with other similar approaches, including agile and six sigma. We will now consider the main concepts and principles behind lean.

CHAPTER 2: LEAN PRINCIPLES AND CONCEPTS

Overview

In the previous chapter we considered some of the key concepts for lean. But how do you actually complete a lean project? What are the tools and how are they used? We will consider these questions in this chapter.

Principles

Lean principles are used to methodically examine business and related processes focusing on customer value and the elimination of waste. The benefits of this approach include:

- Focusing on satisfying customers hence increasing future income streams.
- Identifying and evaluating potential bottlenecks or other problem areas.
- Increasing the efficiency of the organisation.
- Saving money, e.g. by reducing overheads.
- Simplifying processes.
- Being able to demonstrate conformity to internal business rules and external regulatory or reporting requirements.

Another principle often cited with lean is the kaizen philosophy of continuous improvement/change. This is a

Japanese principle based on the following cycle:

1. Standardisation of operation
2. Measurement
3. Comparison of measurement to requirement
4. Make small changes to meet requirements/improve productivity
5. Repeat from step one.

Or to put it another way 'Plan', 'Do', 'Check' and 'Act' (PDCA).

The five key principles

The five key principles for lean:

1. Identify Customers and Specify **Value**
2. Identify and Map the **Value Stream**
3. Create **Flow** by Eliminating Waste
4. Respond to Customer **Pull**
5. Pursue **Perfection**.

These are described below.

Value

In the lean approach, value is defined by the customer – it is hence dependent on the price that they are willing to pay. By implication if it does not have a price it is waste and needs to be minimised. For public sector organisations, e.g. the NHS, it may not be possible to assess value in monetary terms – instead value needs to be assessed as the benefit to the patient or other stakeholders (e.g. their GP). The principle of identifying customers and specifying value will be explored further in *Chapter 3*.

Value stream

This is the core process of activities that deliver the value as identified above. It should cover the full end-to-end process, including all boundaries. So, this could be first contact for a potential sale, from any of a number of different channels, right through to final delivery and payment. There are processes in lean for mapping the value stream (*see Chapter 4*).

Flow

The value stream should flow from end to end with no blockages and with minimal hand-offs to other parties. To achieve this requires batching of activities, removal of processes adding little or no value, and the alignment of demand and capacity/production. A technique known as value stream mapping is used in agile to map existing and intended process flows. This enables the assessment of opportunities for improving flow efficiency, thereby reducing waste and cost (*see Chapter 5*).

Pull

The flow is pulled through the process (rather than being pushed) based on actual customer demand. Traditional production planning was based on estimating demand, both of the type of product needed and volumes. This often results in an insufficient product of the right model or specification being available if demand is higher than expected. Worse still, in some cases too much of the wrong specification can be made, leading to waste and a need to sell the excess at a vastly reduced price (e.g. books via remaindering channels).

In the push model, production is based on the supply of raw materials – with production pushed through each stage as it continues. Any surplus is stored, either at the end of the process or at each stage. In addition to waste, queues can form, where a production step is waiting for missing components. There is often poor synchronisation of these sub-processes, leading to each one working on different products at the same time. Also, the organisation will be failing to provide what the customer values, when they want it.

Instead of the push from raw material to finished product, lean is based on a pull – from the customer demand through the process, back to raw materials, stage by stage *(see Chapter 6)*. Components, or raw materials, are only requested from the previous step by each stage as they are actually required. This enables organisations to produce in line with actual demand at that moment in time. This reduces work in progress stock inventory waste.

Perfection

The level of quality is the value defined by the customer, however, this can change over time as their expectations increase (particularly in a competitive marketplace). For this and other reasons, perfection is therefore an unattainable goal but should still be strived for. The aim of lean thinking is to pursue perfection by continuously improving the process flow, dependent on:

- constant incremental improvements
- best practice and willingness to experiment
- learning
- feedback from customers and other stakeholders
- innovation and technological changes.

(*see Chapter 7*).

Minimise waste

Businesses have to perform many tasks and activities. Some of these add real and direct benefit to the product or service provided. Benefit that the customer can see – a product they can buy, on sale in a way convenient to them, delivered when and where they need it. These are called 'value added activities' and are a good thing.

Businesses also need to undertake other activities to stay in business and operate in a legal way – for example, support board activities, financial accounting, health and safety, IT infrastructure and regulatory/compliance activities. This is referred to as 'incidental work' and can be seen as an overhead to the main activity. As such, they still need to be provided in a way that minimises waste.

If activities are undertaken that do not add real value to the customer, or are required to operate the business, they are referred to as 'non-value added' and can be seen as potential waste.

There are eight areas of waste identified for lean that can be remembered using the acronym 'DOWNTIME':

1. Defects
2. Overproduction
3. Waiting
4. Not utilising talent
5. Transportation
6. Inventory excess
7. Motion waste
8. Excess processing.

Lean approaches and tools

A number of tools, approaches and techniques have been developed to assist with lean projects. Some of these are applied to specific principles (e.g. the Kano model for customer value) and these will be considered in the specific chapter where they apply. Other general tools include:

• value stream mapping
• root cause analysis
  o the 5 Whys
  o fishbone diagrams.

These are described below.

Value stream mapping

All organisations take some form of raw material or basic service, add to it, and then sell on the basis of the value added. This process could be very complex, such as taking metal ore and converting it into steel girders, or it could be as simple as re-selling bought goods in a different marketplace, or performing an audit or software development project. The journey from beginning to end is referred to as a 'value stream' and is key to lean thinking. As a customer, I am not generally interested in how complex or difficult the process is. I am merely interested in the value to me as an individual – and that will determine the price I am willing to pay. So the business needs to balance the costs of operating the process, with the value that I place on the final outcome – hopefully leaving an element of profit for them.

It is wasteful to spend millions of pounds on equipment to produce a limited number of low value items (e.g. paper clips). Likewise, it is unlikely to be worthwhile to spend large sums on new software systems that will only be used by a few who will only receive a very limited benefit.

Toyota were aware of the significance of the value stream and used information and material flow diagrams to represent the process. James Womack, Mike Rother and John Shook brought these together to create *Value Stream Mapping* (Lean Enterprise Institute LEI Workbook *Learning to See* 1998). The five main steps are summarised below.

We will consider the process for identifying and mapping the value chain, and how to audit this process, further in *Chapter 5*.

Root cause analysis

If I don't deal with a weed in my garden it will spread. If I cut it off at ground level, it will grow back again – maybe not there but somewhere else. The same is true of issues and problems we may identify in a lean review. Without identifying the cause, it could spread, even if we deal with the immediate problem. The method of identifying the real cause is referred to as root cause analysis (RCA).

If the lights in my house go out, I can reset the fuse or circuit breaker but without knowing why it tripped or blew and resolving that issue, the problem is only temporarily resolved. The loss of power is referred to as the 'proximate' or 'direct', or immediate cause. A root cause could be manifest in a number of different proximate causes. Resolving the root cause will resolve the proximate cause. NASA have been leading thinkers in the area of RCA. This process involves helping to identify:

- What happened? – including an analysis of all available data
- What led to the occurrence?
- Where it happened – including all locations and timings/timelines.
- How it happened and why it happened.
- What are the likely solutions and how cost-effective will each be?

RCA can be used in response to incidents, as a preventative measure to predict failures, or as part of a lessons learnt exercise.

RCA needs to be conducted in a systematic and robust way – otherwise there is a risk that the root cause identified is not the end of the chain and there are other causes below it. The aim is to permanently resolve the issue in the medium to longer term – not necessarily to find a temporary short term immediate fix.

If auditors report only on the immediate cause and not the root cause they are 'failing to add insights that improve the longer-term effectiveness and efficiency of business processes and thus, the overall governance, risk, and control environment' (see The IIA's International Professional Practices Framework (IPPF) Practice Advisory titled *2320-2: Root Cause Analysis*).

There are a number of techniques for performing RCA. The two most common ones are:

1. The 5 Whys
2. Ishikawa (fishbone) diagram.

The 5 Whys

Taiichi Ohno, of Toyota summed up this approach well:

'Ask "why" five times about every matter.' That's it. The whole approach is based on asking one question ('Why?') repetitively. Each repetition gives additional insights to reach the core of the problem – the root cause – each time getting to a more finite level of detail. The key is to take methodical steps in the process and not to jump to conclusions. This enables resources to be focused on the root cause.

Stating and documenting the problem helps to agree what the actual problem is. Brainstorming is then used to identify the cause of the problem by asking the first 'Why' – the second loop is based on the way to this first response and then the process is repeated until the root cause is found.

The following grid can be used as a template for analysis. In practice we would include more detail. The example is taken from Taiichi Ohno's example of a welding robot that stopped working (see *www.toyota-global.com/ company/toyota_traditions/quality/mar_apr_2006.html*)

Table 2: 5 Whys example

What happened?	Robot stopped working
1. Why did the robot stop?	Circuit overload
2. Why did the circuit overload?	Insufficient bearing lubrication
3. Why was there insufficient bearing lubrication?	Oil pump failure
4. Why did the oil pump fail?	Pump intake clogged
5. Why did the pump intake clog?	No filter on pump

So by fitting and maintaining a pump filter, the problem will be fully resolved.

The 5 Whys are sometimes supplemented by the use of a cause and effect diagram (see Ishikawa diagrams below). The 5 Whys approach is a simple to use and imaginative approach. So simple it always reminds me of the way a 5-year old child may try to wear down their parent when they are refused something they want ('Why can't I have an ice cream?', etc.). It also helps to identify other associated issues that may not yet be apparent, or to connect two issues where the relationship has not yet been identified. It does need to be robustly applied to ensure:

1. The final root cause has been identified.
2. There is minimum bias towards the answer that everyone was expecting.

Ishikawa (fishbone) diagram

The Ishikawa (fishbone) diagram provides a basis for cause and effect analysis to help consider a problem in-depth, to identify and resolve the main cause. The problem is expressed in the form of an effect. The tool helps to identify and record the main causes so that these can be evaluated to find the ones most worthwhile to resolve. This is usually achieved in workshops. The technique was first invented by Professor Kaoru Ishikawa of Tokyo University. The diagrams created resembled the bone structure of a fish.

The tool is very good at discovering causes that may not be immediately apparent. By taking a team approach, it brings in different skills, knowledge and perspectives and allows greater analysis of real root causes. The approach could be:

• identify and obtain consensus on issue
• identify four or more major factors
• brainstorm each of the main categories to identify cause of causes.

The technique is highly structured and can work well but it requires consensus on the definition of the problem. The tool helps to identify multiple causes and highlights connections between them. There is a risk that some factors may be missed so it is often useful to perform a show and tell to get additional viewpoints.

Lean governance

As with agile, there is a risk that project and other activity teams assume that there is no governance requirement for lean activities. However, given the strategic impact on the organisation and the changes that will be made, this is incorrect. There still needs to be governance frameworks to ensure that the objectives are achieved, at reasonable cost and timeline, and that teams work within their (defined and adequate) levels of delegation. There may also be specific legal and regulatory compliance issues to consider. Governance and audit should ensure that these are achieved and that the process of continuous improvement is effective (*see Chapters 9 and 10*).

Audit considerations

When auditing or providing other assurance for a specific lean project or activity, the first step is to consider the questions you would use for any other approach, applying the principles described above. For example:

1. Is there sufficient, but not excessive, project governance that the project will complete in budget and the timelines set, whilst achieving the financial and other business benefits identified?

2. Is the project likely to adversely impact another area of the business?

3. Is the project run in accordance with the organisation's policies, practices, processes/methodology and standards for this type of activity?

Summary

In this chapter we have explored the five main principles for lean (identify customers and specify value, identify and map the value stream, create flow by eliminating waste, respond to customer pull, pursue perfection). We have also considered the significance of lean principles and some of the main tools used for root cause analysis (the 5 Whys and fishbone analysis).

Over the next few chapters we will consider the concepts in more depth.

CHAPTER 3: IDENTIFY AND SPECIFY CUSTOMER VALUE

Introduction

Providing quality services is important not only to the customer but also to the business. Providing poor quality will lead to a loss of reputation and wasteful costs rectifying the fault. In our open economies there is strong competition to attract buyers for most goods and services. Businesses also know it is more expensive to find new customers than to have existing ones return or recommend you to someone else.

The customer perspective of what represents value may be different to that of the provider, so understanding what represents their value is essential to ensure that this can be delivered and that effort is not wasted on developing products and services that do not meet these requirements. Also, this may often include items that are not directly related to the service provided (e.g. the friendliness of reception staff, loyalty programmes and accessibility may all be important for hotels).

Consider a very minor fault on an aeroplane – for example my seat back tray not working properly. To the airline, one or two broken trays on an aeroplane holding over 300 passengers may seem trivial, compared with getting the passengers (and hopefully their baggage) safely and securely a couple of thousand miles. But to passengers – it makes it difficult to eat a meal and may also raise irrational (and incorrect) doubts about how the airline services the aircraft and engines. Hence it could be something of value, especially as the cost of repair will be low.

It's a very worn phrase, but we need to understand the whole of the customer journey from their perspective in order to understand what is important. The problem is that this is very subjective and so it's important to gain a wide variety of views – not just from existing customers but also from prospective customers in a wider market

Customer value

In lean, the term customer value is a relative one, as different customers will have different levels of expectations. For bespoke tailors or others delivering premium personalised services, this may not be an issue, as they can cater to the high value, low volume market by meeting these expectations. But large volume producers may need to have a proxy for what customer's regard as value. Organisations invest a lot of time and effort to understand their customer base and the value, in terms of price they are willing to pay for that good or service. I have been involved in a number of such projects to provide a single view of the customer and data that can be used to profile the customers' requirements or identify other services that we can offer.

Suppliers are trying to hear the voice of the customer and in a lean environment this would be used as a pull for supply and production. However, there are a number of flaws:

1. Suppliers often inadvertently ask for information in a biased way that limits the information they receive

from potential customers. For example, a few years ago I was at an international air show and was asked to undertake a survey. There were ten questions, such as 'Would you prefer to fly direct to your end destination or go via a hub'? The other questions were similar – it was obvious to me that the survey was on behalf of Boeing and was designed to justify not building a super jumbo, rather to compete with the A380.

2. The bias is towards existing customers and what they have bought, based on what the supplier wants to provide. There is little or no information from other potential buyers.

As choices available have increased, the customer has been given more power, as they can often find an alternative product or service. By illustration, let's consider the experience of two customers, both buying bedroom furniture – one in the 1950s and one in the 2010s.

In the 1950s, the customer would go along to their local furniture store, during their limited opening hours, and would have a very limited range to choose from – perhaps just one or two manufacturers. Having made the choice, they would speak to a salesman who would arrange HP credit for them which they would then repay in monthly instalments. There may be some room for negotiation on price but very little – also no scope for changing the design of the furniture, with only a limited number of colours and handles available. The shop would write to the customer when the furniture was available (probably after a couple of months) and delivery and installation of the pre-made furniture would be arranged.

The deliverymen would check the furniture, remove all packaging and perhaps even take away the old furniture being replaced. There was rarely any formal arrangement to provide feedback, other than if the customer went back into the same shop for something else and the salesman remembered them. Overall the input required from the customer was minimal.

In the 2010s the customer can source the furniture from virtually anywhere via the Internet, at a time and place convenient to them. The choice is also almost endless – including pre-owned items. The customer has greater control over the choice and the amount paid – they can bid, compare prices and even to a certain extent negotiate. They may be given some form of 'loyalty' award for items they have bought previously. They may also be able to create a virtual image of their bedroom and see how the furniture would appear, including plans of the room with the new furniture, to see how it fits. Even when the choice has been made, the customer is asked to make choices about colour, design, delivery, etc. The site is then likely to make a number of further recommendations for purchase at the same time (e.g. carpets, linen, coat hangers …). If the customer decides to buy they will be taken online to a payment portal and provide credit card or online payment information. The purchase and payment arrangements have been separated. The customer will then be sent an email confirming the order and providing tracking information – probably within two weeks. They are asked for feedback on the website, including many additional questions relating to demographics and future purchasing requirements. They may also be asked to 'friend' the supplier on social media – even though they have had no human contact with the vendor throughout the process.

When delivery is made, they will need to arrange for someone to be at home when it is delivered. They will then have to take the furniture into the room, unpack the furniture, build it and then dispose of the packaging and the old furniture. They are then asked to complete a survey for the furniture and probably a separate survey for the delivery company. The customer will also receive many more emails in a week informing them of offers, etc. In this scenario the customer has more choice but they have purchased a pile of wood – not the end-to-end service they would have received from the 1950's scenario.

In their book *Lean Solutions: How Companies and Customers can Create Value and Wealth Together*, Womack and Jones identify six principles underpinning lean consumption.

As a customer I want you to:

- completely solve my problem
- not waste my time
- seliver my needs
- deliver value where I want it
- supply value when I want it
- reduce the number of decisions I must make to solve my problem.

Based on the scenario I described above, it would seem that in some ways the customer experience was better in the 1950s than it is today. Hence there is a lot of work that many organisations still need to do to fully understand and emphasise with their customer's true needs.

Key concepts, techniques and tools

Defining value

Value is subjective – not only from the perspective of the customer but also from the perspective of the supplier. The customer will think of the end-to-end experience as constituting value. So, as we saw in the furniture example earlier, this may be not only the actual product, but how it is marketed, sold, delivered and installed and after sales service. A shop selling furniture therefore needs to consider every step of this process – not just the sale. Some organisations seem to have taken this even further. Many utility companies, for example, can have different departments working in silos to provide their specific part of the service. I once called my telephone service provider with an issue and was transferred eight times – the last time back to the first person I had spoken to without the problem being solved – I gave up and just went to another supplier. I have also been told my problem is nothing to do with them as they have outsourced that part of the process! As a customer I am not interested in how you decide to manage the service – I just want to get the value I am paying them for.

The challenge of lean then is for organisations to re-think what constitutes value. This will often be based on guess work, based on the best information available at the time – and it will change over time. This rate of change has increased with the information revolution, as customers can now be better advised and can obtain feedback from other customers and fairly independent review websites on any purchases, from technology, cars, travel, cruises and restaurants – the list is endless. Social media also plays a part – a small family run restaurant had a customer who had a complaint – they resorted to social media and the proprietor of the restaurant made an inappropriate response – this quickly went viral, not only in the local press but also on the wider web, with an impact on the media.

Customer needs

Customers only buy products or services because they have a need. Maslow categorised these in his hierarchy of needs:

Figure 1: Maslow's hierarchy of needs

All suppliers are seeking to meet one or more of the above needs. There are slight variations in the products required for each in different cultures. For example, in the emerging economies there is an increasing demand for red meat products as the population becomes wealthier. There are also changes over time, for example, when they were first invented mobile phones could only be afforded by the wealthy, now they are almost universal.

The Kano model

For a product or service to be successful, it needs to fulfil one or more of the needs identified above, in response to a customer's problem. Professor Noriaki Kano developed the Kano model in 1984 (see *www.kanomodel.com/*) from his studies of customer satisfaction and loyalty. The model is now supported by a number of tools and matrices.

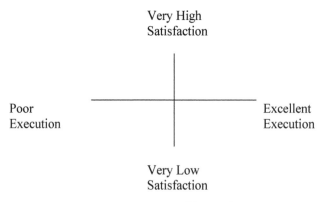

Figure 2: The Kano model

The grid consists of a Y axis (Satisfaction) and an X axis (Execution).

Satisfaction

The Y axis shows satisfaction of the customer, from low at the bottom, to high at the top. This is subjective and will vary between customers and products/services. Because of our expectations as customers, some services will have a neutral impact because we expect them to work. Take buying a washing powder, for example. If I regularly buy a particular brand at a particular price, I will be neutral when I make the purchase – it's just meeting my expectations. I will remain neutral as long as I don't suddenly develop an allergy and the product continues to operate as I expect. However, if I buy a new brand at a lower price than my previous brand and it gets my shirts cleaner, with a nice smell, I will have a higher level of satisfaction. Over time the level of satisfaction may subside and decrease.

There is also some scope creep in society as our expectations increase and this is especially true for software products. There has been an incredible rate of change over the last 30 years. Imagine I am going to launch a spreadsheet competitor to MS Excel – my product has a limit of 20 rows and 20 columns and can only perform basic mathematical functions. I don't think the market would be very excited about this! However, in 1983 we used just such a product and it was brilliant – saving a lot of time over the previous method of pen, analysis paper, paper tape calculator and correcting fluid.

Execution

The X axis represents execution, or fulfilment, from low on the left, to high on the right. These represent how well the provider is able to execute, or meet, the requirement for the goods or service. Execution covers the whole life of the product or service, from initial marketing, production, sales, delivery and post sale support. The scale is from poor to excellent.

Customer preference

Kano used the grid to illustrate three distinct categories of customer preference:

- Performance (as an arrow going from the bottom left to top right box)
- Basic (as an arrow from bottom left to bottom right box)
- Excitement (as an arrow from top left to top right box).

Performance

Performance requirements are those requirements that customers can easily define, articulate, communicate and in some cases measure (e.g. the energy efficiency rating of a household appliance). If these requirements are executed badly, the customer will have a very low level of satisfaction (bottom, left quadrant of the chart). If executed well, they will bring high satisfaction.

On a software project, for example, these will be the requirements identified in the customer requirements or design documentation. They will be used as a basic measure to ensure the software meets its requirements and should be included in testing and product demonstrations, such as show and tells.

Basic

Basic (or 'must-be's') are the requirements that customers expect and assume will be included. When performed well, customers will be neutral (like in my washing powder example above). They do cause dissatisfaction, however, when they are not delivered. We expect that products 'do what they say on the tin' – I expect a glue to stick things, a pen to make a mark, etc.

One issue with basic requirements is that because the customer is expecting them to be delivered they may not be specified clearly by the customer. I have found this a particular problem on software projects, leading to many failures not being identified until user acceptance testing, or even after go live.

Excitement (Wow factor)

These are the nice surprises, the features with benefits that we were not expecting, that differentiate the product or service from its competitors. For example, the flight upgrades we were not expecting, but got as a reward for loyalty, or free postage on a delivery.

On software products, when a standard package has been introduced, there may be features that were not identified in the requirements but still provide benefit. I helped to introduce a new cashier system where the requirement was to 'make it like the old system'. The new version had a bounced cheque warning facility which was particularly helpful to the cashiers when receiving cheques from high-risk customers.

Some innovations and changes can have a reverse effect, where the feature is disliked by the customer base. These should be rare if the supplier has done their customer research – they can usually be seen when the next release or model reverts to the previous functionality. BMW, for example, removed the temperature gauge from the instrument panel of their three series, and then brought it back on the next model due to customer demand. Dissatisfiers are waste, as the supplier is providing a feature that the customer does not see as a benefit – the customer will therefore not pay a premium for the feature and may prefer to purchase a product from another supplier that does not have it.

Audit considerations

The best approach is for the reviewer to identify all potential customers and then list the five key benefits that the customer is considering, and the likely price they will pay compared to competition. This will provide a high-level sense check of the findings reached by management.

The following questions are designed to help review the process that management has followed.

- How have management identified potential customer groups? – both end consumers and intermediaries.
- Has this review recently been reviewed and updated?
- Where do key stakeholders consider they are on the axes of 'Basic'/'Performance' and 'Excitement'?
- What is the current status of complaints received from customers?

- Is there evidence to show that complaints are decreasing and customer satisfaction is increasing due to lean interventions?

Summary

Understanding and responding to customer needs helps to generate new income and reduce waste. Under lean thinking this may require a re-thinking. It will be the basis upon which customer needs are defined and fulfilled, and will need to be re-considered over time as customers' needs and expectations change, and competitors are innovative in their response.

The Kano model helps producers to scientifically understand and document all potential customer requirements or features to prioritise development efforts on the features and benefits that most influence satisfaction and generate future loyalty, thereby adding customer value.

In this chapter we have considered how customer value can be defined and monitored. This is a key part of understanding the lean process, and in the next chapter we will consider how this value is considered throughout the value creation process.

Another consideration for suppliers will be the target cost – can they meet these expectations and deliver at a price expected by the customer? In a lean organisation this will involve the reduction of waste and other costs to achieve the price required. We will consider this process further in the next chapter on the value stream.

CHAPTER 4: IDENTIFY AND MAP VALUE STREAM

Introduction

In the previous chapter we considered what customers value and how this is determined. The next stage in lean thinking is to consider the processes by which this value is delivered and fulfilled. This value stream starts with raw material, or a service idea, right through to fulfilment to the final consumer. Lean has a process for considering and documenting this in the form of a 'value stream map'.

Value stream mapping

Lean considers each step of the production process, analysing in terms of the value added for the customer from the start to finish of the process. These are mapped to allow analysis – the focus on value stream mapping is to identify waste (including rework, scrappage and set up times). The map is a visual representation identifying each step.

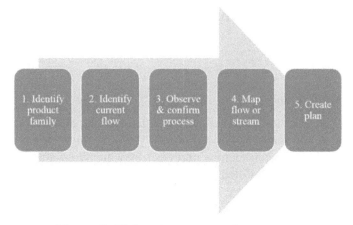

Figure 3: Value stream mapping process

Each of these five steps are described below.

Step 1. Identify product family

The first step is to identify which products are to be included in the value stream to be reviewed. This step sets the scope for the mapping exercise. Generally, this will be based upon products which pass through similar process steps. The focus should be on higher value/volume processes.

At this stage it is also important to identify all of the locations where the specified product family is processed. It is also necessary to have an understanding of the goals and objectives to be achieved and any known issues.

Step 2. Identify current flow

An initial map will be prepared on the 'as is' or current state. There are a number of ways this can be prepared, including:

- Using existing process flows and swim lanes.
- Walking through the process using the customer journey perspective.
- Reviewing previous customer feedback to identify which steps are of most value to them.
- Drawing the process and validating with key stakeholders.
- Document each procedural step with high-level notes and examples of transactions (showing for each the inputs, processes and outputs). May also include the 'customer' and 'supplier', even if these are internal to the organisation.
- Highlighting areas of known potential improvement in the process.
- Obtaining relevant benchmark, the key performance indicators (KPIs) for the process, which may include:
  o volumes – both stock and flow over time
  o frequency
  o error rates/quality failures
  o time to complete – in total and broken down by process steps
  o variations in customer demand (e.g. seasonal peaks and troughs)
  o available production time/required units of production. So if there are seven working hours in a

day (after allowing for breaks, etc.) and the customer demand is seven units, the take time would be one hour.

• Using information flows.

Step 3. Observe and confirm process

The mapping begins with a 'gemba' walk (Japanese word meaning 'the real place'). This is a walkthrough of the location where the process is performed. This can be the factory floor, warehouse or office. It is easier to identify waste from seeing the process in action. Also, the flowcharts and other documentation prepared by management may not cover the current process in practice, or may not be applied consistently across different sites. By visiting different locations operating the same process, it is also often possible to identify areas of best practice, some of which may not be identifiable from the KPIs gathered during step two above. Often the mapping will commence at the end – the point at which the product or service is despatched to the customer. It then continues back up the value stream. The output from this step will be process documentation and other evidence (e.g. samples of product at each stage, photographs, QA reports) to support the process documentation.

Step 4. Map the flow or stream

Unlike other forms of process mapping, workshops would not normally be run to draw and confirm the process until the above has been completed. This is when the large rolls of brown paper are used to complete the process map.

The current flow can then be analysed to identify those steps which are:

1. Value adding activities – Those which create value for the customer for which they are willing to pay.
2. Non value adding activities – Those which do not add customer value and there are no bars to them being eliminated immediately.
3. Value enabling activities – Those which do not create direct value, but cannot be eliminated or changed at this stage, usually because they are required for related processes (type 1 Muda). May also include items, such as health and safety, or IT security/data privacy.

Where there are bottlenecks identified in the process, the technique of 'heijunka' may be used to smooth the flow. This aims to level the type and quantity of production over a time, to respond to the pull from customers, avoiding batching and large stock levels, without the corresponding capital and staffing costs.

Step 5. Creating the (implementation) plan

A future state map is then created of the ideal value flow – to exclude areas of waste, including reducing the time for processing if possible. This forms the basis for a project plan to move the desired flow – with reduced waste/cost and more streamlining. There should also be increased quality for the customer, which could be measured using the Kano model described in the previous chapter.

Tools for value stream mapping

To support the five steps for value stream mapping described above, there is an established toolbox with seven components:

1. Process activity mapping
2. Supply chain responsiveness matrix
3. Production variety funnel
4. Quality filter mapping
5. Demand amplification mapping
6. Decision point analysis
7. Physical structure mapping.

This is based on the work defined by Hines and Rich (see Peter Hines, Nick Rich, (1997) *The Seven Value Stream Mapping Tools*, International Journal of Operations & Production Management, Vol. 17 Issue: 1). These tools have been collated from a number of different sources and backgrounds including academia, manufacturing and engineering.

A brief overview of each of these is given below. It is unlikely that all of these tools would be encountered on a particular project. I have included them here for completeness.

There is an excellent illustration of how these tools are applied in practice for a foundry operation by Pude and Naik (see IOSR Journal of Mechanical and Civil Engineering (IOSR-JMCE) ISSN: 2278-1684, PP: 07-12). This illustrates the use of some of the tools to review production in a metal foundry.

Tool 1: Process activity mapping

Process activity mapping is a tool to map the whole of a production process, from receiving raw materials up to the fulfilment of the customer's order. The maps help to identify and analyse lead time and opportunities to improve production/reduce waste. Every step of the process is mapped, including the supply chain sub-processes. Mapping is completed in five steps:

1. Map and study process flow
2. Identify potential waste
3. Consider changing sequences of process
4. Consider alternative process flow patterns
5. Consider whether all actions at each stage are necessary, and the implications of removing specific tasks.

This determines the main components of the process and documents a process map. It can include a number of metrics. For each step key considerations are:

- Who performs it?
- What resources and tools are used?
- Why the activity occurs (based on customer value)?
- Where it occurs?
- When it occurs?
- How often it occurs?

The above steps also help to identify any duplicate or missing activity in the process, and wastage due to unnecessary hand-offs between different people performing tasks.

Process activity mapping could be applied to a software project. By understanding the flow of the project, including any quality stage gates, the project plan could be streamlined. For example, by identifying any unnecessary, wasteful or duplicated steps, or improving the hand-offs between different sub-teams.

Tool 2: Supply chain responsiveness matrix (SCRM)

The supply chain responsiveness matrix (SCRM) is an inventory management tool used to analyse stock levels with their process and lead times. As spend on raw materials and input services can be a very high proportion of spend (depending on the industry sector), also tying up working capital or requiring short term credit, it is important to ensure that excessive stock levels are not held. However, there is a risk of stock outages if the stock levels are too low for just in time production, leading to idle time waste. The SCRM is usually shown in an easy to use graphical form, with the inventory time shown on the Y axis and the lead time shown on the X axis. The chart enables process teams to focus on areas with excessive stock holdings, or where other improvements can be made. In some cases, apparent overstocking may be unavoidable – for example in the potato snacks industry the main raw material, potatoes, is seasonally harvested, whilst demand for the end product is fairly uniform throughout the year.

This tool could also be applied for software projects. I have known several projects to be delayed because the supporting software or releases were not yet available, or due to offshore testing, or other third party activities not being completed. Using the SCRM approach could help to reduce these potential delays.

Tool 3: Production variety funnel

Different end product variants will require different components to be created – the production variety funnel is a way of identifying these variations at each production stage, and then presenting the result in a chart form. This helps to identify issues around the number of variations and whether there are opportunities for standardisation. The maps can also be used to find where the stock can be held most beneficially during processing, based on likely levels of demand.

Standardisation of sub-components can have benefits to the customer, as well as in the future maintenance of the project. For example, the 'hand-built' nature of the Nimrod reconnaissance aircraft made them expensive and difficult to maintain, as standard components could not be used. This led ultimately to their scrapping. In the Apollo 13 incident, air filters built for the lunar module of the space craft had to be 'modified' during the flight home, to be useable in the main capsule.

This tool could also be used on software projects. For example, using a modular approach in a system means that modules can be re-used elsewhere in the system, helping to reduce waste and provide a more standard user interface and ease of future maintenance.

Tool 4: Quality filter mapping

Defects can occur throughout a process, however, defects in individual components may not become apparent until later in production. This causes additional waste, as the additional processing performed may not have been necessary. For example, faulty raw materials in a food processing factory could cause the whole batch of production to be scrapped. Quality filter mapping helps to identify where defects occur and where they are discovered.

Quality filter mapping looks at three areas of quality:

1. Product quality – the quality of the end product or service provided to the customer. This will be represented by product returns or complaints.
2. Defects found (scrap) – these are the defects found during production quality control, which were either remedied or led to waste.
3. Service quality – these are issues impacting the ability to provide the product to the customer (e.g. failure of a piece of machinery vital to the process).

Quality filter mapping considers the failure rates for each of these as a ratio (e.g. parts per million/thousand/ hundred) for each stage of production.

Quality filter mapping could be applied to software projects, testing to ensure that faults are corrected as soon as possible.

Tool 5: Demand amplification mapping

Sudden changes in customer demand, or changes required in later stages of production, can have a ripple effect back through the process. It's like the effect of a car braking slightly on a highway – the cars behind all brake increasingly harder, leaving the cars at the back to possibly actually stop. Likewise, in a production cycle a change in orders received, for example, could have an increasing impact back through the process. This phenomenon is known as 'demand amplification', or the Forrester Effect (after Jay W Forrester who mathematically documented it in the 1950s at Massachusetts Institute of Technology.

It is also sometimes called the bullwhip effect, as the amplitude of the impact increases as it progresses through the supply chain, in a similar way to the cracking of a whip. In addition to changes in demand, the effect can also be caused by changes and adjustments to products during the processes.

The demand amplification chart (aka the Forrester effect chart) shows the level of variation in demand at each stage or time interval for the production process.

Tool 6: Decision point analysis

The decision point in a process stream is that point where the customer pull in the process is exceeded by the push of production. At this point, products or components are being created based on forecast, or other issues not related to the actual level of demand at that time. Where we are aiming to have production based on customer pull, an understanding of where this occurs is vital to assess processes either side of the point, to ensure alignment with the push or pull. Also, by considering changes in scenarios, the impact of a move of the decision point can be considered, allowing improved design of the value stream.

This is one of the lesser used of the seven tools. There has been some application in the childcare arena in the US.

Tool 7: Physical structure mapping

Physical structure mapping is used to provide an oversight of how the production process fits within the industry as a whole. This provides an understanding of the operation of the supply and demand side of the industry, and can highlight opportunities where there has so far been little consideration by competitors. The tool is in two graphical parts:

1. Volume structure – this shows the number of organisations in the industry structure in which the producer operates, broken down into tiers for supply (raw materials and support) and distribution, including after sales support.

2. Cost structure – this is based on the same organisations shown in the volume structure, but is based on the value added by each. This can be compared to the value added to identify potential unneeded or unrewarding steps in the entirety of the process, so waste can be reduced.

Lean project within mapping stream

One area to consider may be the impact of the project itself on the overall value stream. The conduct of the project should be invisible to the end customer until it actually delivers some benefit. I find it very frustrating as a customer to be told that my requirements cannot be met because the 'system is being upgraded', or that the product has been withdrawn because a new model is due out shortly.

Summary and audit approach

The toolkit is a useful way to identify potential tools to understand the value stream process. Like any tool, it is important to ensure that their use is appropriate for the objectives of the review or project. The overall aim of lean thinking is to identify waste, ensure continuous improvement and maximise value to the customer. Any tools used should hence be focused on achieving this objective.

The following audit questions will assist in any review:

1. How has the impact upon the entire value stream been considered?

2. What tools have been used to document the value stream?

3. Are the tools used appropriately and will they be applied effectively?

4. What evidence is there that the output from the tools has been reviewed and opportunities identified for waste reduction, continuous improvement or adding customer value?

5. How has the use of the tools been evaluated?

Having mapped the existing value flow, the next lean principle considers the creation of future flows to eliminate waste. This is considered in the next chapter.

CHAPTER 5: CREATE FLOW BY ELIMINATING WASTE

Introduction

Waste inhibits flow. This is true of litter on motorways, 'fatbergs' in sewers, excessive production being kept in warehouses, or IT programmers being asked to write code that is not needed and will never be used. Other examples include excessive emails and meetings. In all these cases the normal flow has been interrupted because of waste.

By eliminating waste, we speed the process of transforming raw material into customer value. Waste is also uncompetitive, because if we have waste that competitors do not, they will be able to go to market quicker and with lower costs. Indeed, a unique selling proposition for new entrants may be that they find a way of avoiding waste that others have yet to find.

Waste is also about putting effort into doing the wrong things. A number of projects I see are in danger of producing systems which make the same mistakes as the previous ones – only faster and in larger volumes. Improving the efficiency of being ineffective. As Peter Drucker stated 'There is nothing quite so useless as doing with great efficiency what should not be done at all'. (*http://hbswk.hbs.edu/archive/5377.html*).

Eight areas of waste

In this chapter we will consider the eight wastes identified in *Chapter 2* and consider some tools and techniques to improve flow by removing these areas of waste. We will also consider the tools used in lean to help eliminate waste (gemba walks, reduce/reuse/recycle, just in time and batch size reduction).

The eight areas are:

1. Defects
2. Overproduction
3. Waiting
4. Not utilising talent
5. Transportation
6. Inventory excess
7. Motion waste
8. Excess processing.

Even where waste does occur, there is an opportunity to learn from it and improve our approach next time. I like the lean/agile concept of 'failing early' – in my opinion early failure is not failure at all. If there is learning and change of action/behaviours – it can be success in avoiding larger mistakes. My degree is in science and the scientific principle of experimentation is important – the failures can sometimes lead to new discoveries – for example Fleming's discovery of Penicillin.

By examining the process flow for each of the waste types, it is possible to develop a risk heat map to show where the highest risk of a waste occurring and its greatest impact will be.

These are summarised in *Table 3*.

Table 3: Eight areas of waste

Waste area	Explanation	Examples
1. Defects	Mistakes cost time and effort to rectify and can lead to customer dissatisfaction	1. Poor testing or QA prior to despatch 2. Lack of standards 3. Incomplete or inaccurate documentation 4. Misunderstanding customer expectations
2. Overproduction	Producing too much, sooner or faster than is needed –leading to increased need for working capital, or that the resource used could have been better applied elsewhere	1. Creating products that are outdated and not saleable 2. Printing too many copies of documentation 3. Creating software features no one will use 4. Just in case purchasing
3. Waiting	Work has to stop because of resourcing/supply issues	1. Workflow delays (e.g. awaiting approvals) 2. Production bottlenecks 3. Meetings starting late

Waste area	Explanation	Examples
		4. Waiting delivery from previous sub-process 5. Failure to implement an effective just in time approach
4. Not utilising talent	Not fully using the skills, talents and knowledge of staff and other business partners	1. Hiring new staff or consultants to provide skill sets already available 2. Not listening to suggestions made by workforce 3. Over-restricting responsibilities and authorisations 4. Delays in fully rolling out technology or processes 5. Inadequate briefing and training
5. Transportation	Waste caused by having to move, or handle, components or work packages between stages	1. Storage of files or inventory too remote from where it will be needed 2. Slow delivery processes

Waste area	Explanation	Examples
6. Inventory excess	Excessive storing of components or finished product	1. Agile deliverable product not yet deployed 2. Out of date components 3. Licences for software no longer used
7. Motion waste	Unnecessary physical movement	1. Tools or components not readily available when needed 2. Misplacing documents or making them hard to find in shared team sites 3. Premature archiving
8. Excess processing	Process steps that are duplicated or otherwise unnecessary to achieve customer value	1. Over burdensome reporting 2. Needless bureaucracy/red tape 3. Repeating work already performed 4. Process steps that do not consider current requirements or technology

Another way to consider the eight areas of waste is to look at the associated risks, their common causes and some controls that would help to reduce the likelihood and impact of each risk. This approach is illustrated in *Table 4*.

Table 4: The eight areas of waste

Waste area	Risk overview	Common causes	Suggested controls
1. Defects	Mistakes cost time and effort to rectify and can lead to customer dissatisfaction	Poor quality control Not performing root cause for errors found in quality control failures – keep repeating error	Monitoring/ QA at point of production
2. Over-production	Producing too much, sooner or faster than is needed – leading to increased need for working capital, or that the resource used could have been better applied elsewhere	Failure to allow pull based on customer demand Poor prediction of customer demand	Better prediction of demand based on past patterns and likely future trends

Waste area	Risk overview	Common causes	Suggested controls
3. Waiting	Work has to stop because of resourcing/ supply issues	Changes to workflow not being reflected in workspace structure Poor planning	Process mapping and restricting of workspace to allow better flow between steps (could include data storage)
4. Not utilising talent	Not fully using the skills, talents and knowledge of staff and other business partners	Lack of awareness of skills available Overly hierarchical structures	Skills audits Suggestion schemes
5. Transpor- tation	Waste caused by having to move, or handle, components or work packages between stages	Poor location	Process maps following the flow of product/ service
6. Inventory excess	Excessive storing of components or finished product	Poor production planning	Review and reduce stock levels

Waste area	Risk overview	Common causes	Suggested controls
7. Motion waste	Unnecessary physical movement	Poor design of workspace	Process mapping and restricting of workspace to allow better flow between steps (could include data storage)
8. Excess processing	Process steps that are duplicated or otherwise unnecessary to achieve customer value	Poor understanding of what customers value. Outdated production techniques	Steps to understand customer value and review of competitor activity to identify best behaviours

Key concepts, techniques and tools

Gemba

One of my previous colleagues encouraged me to always ask for a walk of the facility whenever I went to a new client. Very good advice. The Japanese have a word for this, 'gemba' – the place where 'the real work' is done.

We talk about 'the customer journey' but how often do we take this journey to see what life is like in the customer's shoes? A lot of waste areas and customer frustrations can be avoided if we do. I found this technique extremely useful when project managing the implementation of an online service. Show and tell sessions are much more powerful when conducted from the customer's perspective.

The number of times we try to perform our work without a thorough understanding of what is actually happening. The descriptions of processes by management are often out of date and are not always reflective of what happens in the project office or on the factory floor.

At my first visit to one client on a project review, we were met at reception. Security was good but the reception area was disorganised and messy. We walked to the first office where the business representatives sat. There were no posters, time charts, etc. to spark any excitement about the project they were on (a very important strategic one), people stood around talking and there was no sense of urgency (three weeks before go live!). The development staff were in a completely different building. So before we had even reached the meeting room, I already had some ideas about where the project was going wrong.

Reduce/recycle/re-use

During my career there has been a big increase in social and environmental awareness. Waste costs businesses money and can also have a reputational impact. Disposal of waste is becoming more expensive with the imposition of landfill taxes. Various exposes of waste in the food industry have been detrimental to the reputations of some of the supermarket chains and have led to changes in behaviour of the companies concerned, their suppliers and customers. The mantra of Reduce> Recycle> Reuse, rather than Refuse (as in trash or garbage), is a useful one to consider when deciding what to do about waste.

'Reduce' in a lean context is obvious – we should only be producing what the customer needs, in a way that reduces the amount of raw material and consumables required.

'Recycle' in lean means identifying excess from one part of the process that can be applied in another. For example, recycling excess glass or broken jars in a jar making factory. Often it just requires imagination. In some industries recycling is compulsory. For example, the mobile phone industry has to comply with WEEE legislation to ensure phones are removed effectively. This has led to the creation of whole new support industries.

'Reuse' means finding an alternative use for the waste. One man's rubbish can often be another man's treasure. This could be in finding an alternative market for misshaped products, for example providing food to foodbanks, or using waste from the meat industry in pet foods.

Even where waste has been reduced, it is often impossible to eliminate it completely. Some processes will have by-products that are unavoidable. The pursuit of perfection can also mean it is better to reject a product rather than to try to sell it to the customer (John West Salmon once had an advertising slogan 'It's the fish we reject that makes our salmon the best'.).

Just in time

The process flow can often be improved by ensuring that the right resources are available just in time (JIT) – not too early, as this can represent waste in the form of excessive inventory and the associated costs, and not too late, as this will cause waste in the form of process delays. This concept also applies to the distribution of the end product. It is based on research by Taiichi Ohno, one of the founders of lean thinking, based on research at retailers.

JIT theory combines statistical analysis, human behaviours and production management. The costs of carrying inventory are the main driver to identify potentially excessive stock levels. Material also needs to be available at the location and time required, so there is a heavy reliance on good communications and logistics of supply based on demand (as defined by customer pull). Behaviourally, this requires a lot of confidence and support across the supply chain to let go of the traditional, comfort blanket of holding higher stock levels. Hence change is likely to be based on a gradual reduction over time (kaizen) rather than a sudden change (kaikaku).

Batch size reduction (small lot production)

Production in smaller lots or batches can shorten the lead time for production, allowing producers to respond more quickly to changes in demand. This is because small batches can be ready for use immediately, just in time, rather than waiting for the completion of a larger batch. Where goods are perishable or date limited, this can also reduce waste. This is particularly true for productions based on a number of variants of the component or product. It is a critical component of the just in time approach described above, with a focus on reducing waste.

A key consideration may be set up time – if the set up time for a component is long compared to the average production time per item, production of smaller batches could lead to additional waste in the longer term.

This concept is very similar to the agile concept of small, frequent, incremental changes that can be more easily released and assimilated into business processes.

Audit approach

The auditor could perform a gemba style waste walk to understand the process. I have found this an excellent way to understand the process and to get to know auditees better.

As an auditor, a gemba walk is a fantastic way of improving your understanding of a process. When performing a gemba walk I use the acronym 'LACE' (Look>Ask>Change>Evaluate):

Look – clearly observe what is going on and compare this to what you have been told – are there indications of waste, is the site secure? Are the people happy and engaged?

Ask – never be afraid to ask dumb questions – they often lead to interesting answers. Your viewpoint as someone seeing the process for the first time will be different to that of those who have evolved the process.

Change – don't be afraid to make recommendations on the spot – if it's a good idea, and the organisation is set on lean thinking, it could well be adopted or implementation started before you have completed the walk.

Evaluate – walks can be very quick and sometimes you do not have time to evaluate what you have seen – so I always try to repeat the walk in my mind to see if there is anything I may have missed. You could also use the eight wasters (downtime) to see if you have any further recommendations.

When auditing a project, you may wish to perform additional gembas – for example, a project for the release of a new product could include separate gembas of the project office, factory floor and a customer gemba.

Table 5 includes some useful questions to gain insight into the way organisations identify and resolve issues. The questions are based on a manufacturing process, but could be modified for software development or another project. For example, where there is reference to inventory, this could also be systems not yet deployed, or redundant code that is no longer required.

Table 5: Audit of eight areas of waste

Waste area	Explanation	Suggested audit questions
1. Defects	Mistakes cost time and effort to rectify and can lead to customer dissatisfaction	How are QA processes performed and evidenced? Are there adequate KPIs to identify where in the process defects arise? Are common causes of returns (or post go live defects) analysed? How are defects subject to a root cause analysis, in order to identify and resolve their true causes?
2. Overproduction	Producing too much, sooner or faster than is needed – leading to increased need for working capital, or that the resource used could have been better applied elsewhere	How are inventory levels monitored and reviewed? What steps are taken to resolve excess inventory?

Waste area	Explanation	Suggested audit questions
3. Waiting	Work has to stop because of resourcing/supply issues	How are the costs of delays identified? How are process bottlenecks identified and resolved?
4. Not utilising talent	Not fully using the skills, talents and knowledge of staff and other business partners	How are skills audits undertaken (including frequency scope and coverage)? If possible, review personnel files (or professional social media) to identify relevant additional skills of the team
5. Transportation	Waste caused by having to move, or handle, components or work packages between stages	How have transportations been mapped and measured? Are arrangements for co-sourcing and offshoring adequate?
6. Inventory excess	Excessive storing of components or finished product	How much inventory is held relative to current expected levels of use/sale?

Waste area	Explanation	Suggested audit questions
7. Motion waste	Unnecessary physical movement	How are teams co/located? How are workflows reviewed to identify excessive movement (e.g. to identify where steps could be run concurrently)?
8. Excess processing	Process steps that are duplicated or otherwise unnecessary to achieve customer value	How are reporting and governance steps reviewed to ensure that they are required and that they mitigate actual risks? How are steps reviewed to ensure they add customer value?

Summary

This chapter has considered the common causes of waste and how they impact flow. The responsibility of identifying waste should be with all concerned – there are some excellent examples of where waste has been reduced following suggestions from team members. In these cases the benefit needs to be shared with those concerned, to encourage further innovation.

5. *Create Flow by Eliminating Waste*

Having improved the flow through the process it is now important to ensure that this flow is created by a pull from the customers, rather than a push from the producer organisation. A push approach is likely to create further waste. Customer pull will be explored in the next chapter.

CHAPTER 6: RESPOND TO CUSTOMER PULL

Introduction

Imagine you are running a sandwich shop. At the start of each day you could use all your ingredients and create lots of sandwiches – you would then be ready for any customers and be able to serve them immediately. The downside is that you don't know exactly what the customers want to order – so you may have used the wrong ingredients to meet demand – for example you may have made lots of ham and cheese sandwiches and then a bus load of vegetarians arrive wanting only cheese! You would be left with a lot of stock at the end of the day that you needed to dispose of – leading to unnecessary waste.

Alternatively, you could prepare a small stock of your bestselling sandwiches, and then make the sandwiches to order depending on customer preference as customers request them. This is referred to in lean as 'production-pull'. This means no one upstream in the process should produce goods or services, including components, until someone downstream (either a customer or the next processing step) requests them.

Now consider the purchase of a book – I could visit every bookshop to see if they have the title I need. This is time consuming for me and would require each bookshop to have the widest range of books available. Or they could have regional stocks and when I want a particular title they could aim to get it to me within a few days. This is referred to as 'distribution pull'.

Like most publishers, ITGP now have a process for printing books on demand – this one included. In the past, publishers have had to predict the level of demand for a particular title – especially in paperback with the increased use of e-books. Where they have overestimated demand, the books have ended up being remaindered in low price bookstores or pulped. This concept of just in time printing, based on customer demand, was predicted in 'lean thinking'.

Key concepts, techniques and tools

The two different models, traditional push and lean pull, are illustrated in *Figures 4* and *5*.

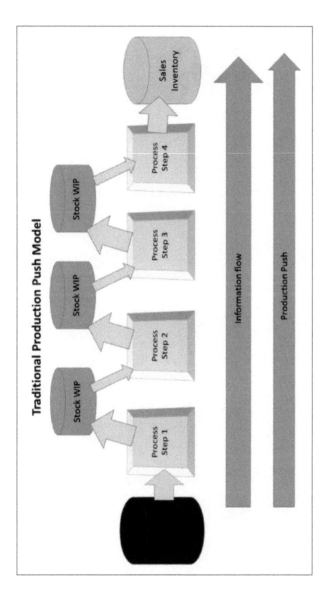

Figure 4: Traditional push model

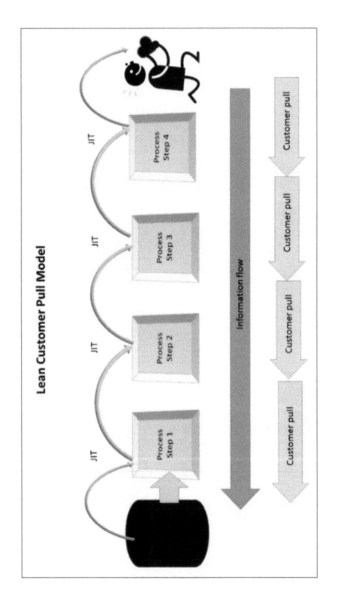

Figure 5: Lean pull model

The diagrams show:

Production push

- Each step makes it into stock/WIP
- Changes in demand are hidden behind rising stock levels spread through the process
- Production may not be based on the type or volume required at that time.

Customer pull

- Every step only makes what is needed next
- Pull is into an empty production slot at each step
- Quicker impact of changes in demand (or production)
- May not be for a specific customer but only hold realistic stock levels
- The pull impacts the whole chain, right back to raw materials
- Production planned based on demand.

For the pull to be effective at each stage, significant levels of data and information need to be gathered, including:

- where the batch is in the process, and whether any blocks are being encountered
- the needs, desires and expectations of customers and what they consider to be of value. This applies not only for the end customer but also for the 'intermediary' customers – i.e. those waiting further along the production chain.

One way to achieve this is the use of a 'kanban' approach, which we will discuss next.

The management of customer information is important in understanding the pull through the process. Many organisations have invested large sums in their customer relationship management (CRM) and related systems to achieve this.

Using kanban to trace batches through the process

A common way of tracing batches through the process whilst ensuring customer pull is the use of kanban (Kan = Card, Ban = Signal). Kanban is not a planning or scheduling tool but can be used for production control.

Using kanban, we would consider the process flow in the customer pull diagram (*see Figure 6*) as a board with a column for each step of the process, and we would add slots beneath to hold the 'cards' (these can be virtual in a system rather than physical cards). *Figure 6* shows a simplified representation of how this could appear.

Status	Proc 1	Proc 2	Proc 3	Proc 4	Dispatched
WIP		Ord 6	Ord 4	Ord 3	
Ready	Ord 7	Ord 5	Ord 3a	Ord 2	Ord 1

Figure 6: Example kanban board phase 1

This is a simplification but it demonstrates the process. Each of the cards in the slots contains additional information about the requirement (e.g. product type, customer if known, date and time at each stage, etc.). In the diagram we can see that there are two empty work in progress slots (process 1 and despatch). The key one from a lean perspective is the despatch slot. We can see that Ord 2 has completed process 4 and is ready for the next stage. By moving this card (and the item) into despatch, we create a new free slot, at 'ready' process 4 – let's assume that Ord 3 is now completed. The updated board would now look like that shown in *Figure 7*:

Status	Proc 1	Proc 2	Proc 3	Proc 4	Dispatched
WIP		Ord 6	Ord 4		Ord 2
Ready	Ord 7	Ord 5	Ord 3a	Ord 3	Ord 1

Figure 7: Example kanban board phase 2

The empty work in progress slot is now at Proc 4 and Ord 3a can now be put into that slot and moved to that process step. The chain reaction can then be repeated.

The board provides an effective visualisation of what is happening in the process in real time. The empty slots are as important as the cards themselves, as they indicate potential for work to enter that phase of the process.

As well as facilitating flow, the use of kanban helps to identify where there are problems or bottlenecks in the process so that these can be investigated and resolved.

Kanban has six associated practices:

1. Visualise (with a kanban board as described above)
2. Limit work in progress (with kanban cards)

3. Manage flow

4. Make policies explicit (e.g. what does complete or 'done' mean?)

5. Implement feedback loops – based on effective monitoring

6. Improve collaboratively and evolve experimentally.

Building a kanban system is complex, as it involves an understanding of the process flows. The risk in some organisations is that they copy a kanban system they have seen elsewhere – this rarely works. I refer to this as the 'John Frum Cult'. This is a cult in the Pacific Ocean that believe by building mock runways and control towers the US GIs will return and bring back the prosperity they brought with them during the Second World War. Copying the kanban system which has been developed for a specific process will not work in a different environment. Many other factors need to be considered, including demand patterns, the maturity of the process and business risks.

Kanban includes a methodology for implementation of kanban – the 'systems thinking approach to introducing kanban' (STATIK). Before commencing, it is important to understand the purpose and objectives of the system or process under review. There are then six steps to STATIK:

1. Understand the motivation for change and sources of dissatisfaction with the current process. This includes personal views of participants and customers, and an analysis of disruptions, interruptions, quality, etc.

2. Analyse the demand (including by type, volume and seasonality) and capability (current capacity and production levels).

3. Model the knowledge discovery/workflow – looking at what knowledge is required for each stage and where this can be obtained from.

4. Discover classes of service – look at different customer expectations, the risk and benefits of each, and then ensure that these are understood by all contributors throughout the process.

5. Design a kanban system, including visualisation.

6. Roll out.

For collaborative improvement, kanban also has four values:

1. Start with what you do now

2. Agree to pursue evolutionary change

3. Initially respect existing roles

4. Encourage acts of leadership at all levels.

Customer information

To ensure effective pull from customers, information is needed about their likely demands. This could be based, for example, on weather forecasts, to know what stock types retailers will need – strawberries and cream for a nice summer's day and soups and warm drinks if there is a cold snap.

Most organisations have also implemented customer relationship management systems to enable them to:

- provide information about the demographic and buying patterns of their customers.
- communicate with customers about new products and offers

- segment the customer base to focus more on higher value customers.

- be able to deal more effectively with complaints and issues in order to maintain a good relationship.

- request feedback and comments on the quality of goods and services provided, including seeking views about planned changes.

There are limitations with this approach, including:

- Information is based only on existing customer base, and what they have historically bought. It provides very little information about what they may have bought (for example if the store had stocked other items).

- Data is often out of date or incomplete.

- Invalid assumptions may be made ('customer who bought new skateboard also bought bandages ... ').

- Risk of SPAM overloading of customers.

- Data privacy concerns.

One solution has been for retailers, and others, to introduce loyalty schemes under which customers are trading information about themselves and their shopping habits in return for regular rewards. One illustration of this is that national chains of retailers now often stock different lines on different days or in different locations, or allow customers to order and receive the goods the following day, if they are not immediately available in the store of their choice.

Audit approach

An audit of customer pull could be based on the STATIK principles as illustrated in *Table 6*.

Table 6: An audit of customer pull based on the STATIK principles

1. What processes are in place to:
a. understand the motivation for change and sources of dissatisfaction
b. analyse the demand
c. model the knowledge discovery/workflow
d. discover classes of service
e. design a kanban system, including visualisation
f. roll out.
2. Has the process been clearly mapped and documented? Is there a risk of misinterpretation of the intended process due to ambiguity?
3. What evidence is there to support the process for each of the above?
4. How is information gathered from customers used to manage the process flow?
5. Perform a (gemba) walk through of the process in both directions.

Summary

Customer pull should pervade throughout the production and distribution process. Kanban provides mechanisms to manage the associated flow of processing and information.

CHAPTER 7: PURSUE PERFECTION

'If your weapon is only 99% perfect, you have a 1% chance of it letting you down when you need it most.' – Kailash Limbu 'Gurkha', Abacus 2015

Introduction

Having considered the first four principles of lean, the fifth one relates to the pursuit of perfection by continuous (incremental) improvement. Perfection is like an elusive target, or an end point on a journey that keeps moving the closer we get to it! This is because of:

- Perceptions of perfection change over time – competitors will find a different way of doing something, or new technologies can be exploited.
- By making changes, new opportunities for change become apparent.
- Sometimes we get a change wrong and it does not have the effect we were expecting – hence we need to make a different change.

The search for perfection needs to include cultural change. The aim is to:

- Wow ALL customers – standing out from competitors.
- Develop a positive environment where staff are happy but strive to do more, by being more aware of customer value and being creative, and being able to constructively challenge assumptions and existing ways of working/areas of waste.

This will form the basis for a total quality management (TQM) system.

The first stage is for the senior stakeholders to agree a vision of what perfection currently looks like for them. They then review where they are at present to understand the size of the gap. If this gap is significant, a plan will be needed to undertake a major series of projects and programmes to narrow this gap (referred to as kaikaku – see below). Following this, or if the gap is not too great, a series of ongoing changes need to be made to ensure that the organisation gets close to the ultimate goal of perfection (kaizen).

One way of showing perfection is to be able to demonstrate a clean and tidy work environment that is well structured and methodical. Lean also has a tool for this – the '5Ss' (see later in the chapter). When people visit the McLaren Technology Group workshops in Woking they comment on how clean and well presented the offices are, with excellent storage of tools and spares to hand for the technicians (see *www.mclaren.com*). The floors and walls are all the same colour grey (Ron Dennis's favourite colour – his personal aircraft has the same colour scheme).

TQM – Total quality management

Many organisations committed to improving quality on a continuous basis adopt the TQM approach, to improve quality at all levels of their organisation. TQM is particularly attuned to the lean objectives of maximising customer value whilst minimising waste. The definition of quality is therefore that defined by the customer – with the organisation aiming to meet, or exceed, the expectation of existing and new customers. Like the rest of lean, the TQM concepts can be applied to any service or product based organisation adopting lean thinking.

TQM originated in the 1950s and has been developed by W Edwards Deming and others (_www.deming.org/theman/theories/fourteenpoints_. Although Deming did not use the phrase 'TQM', the 14 principles in his book _Out of the Crisis_ are widely regarded as a basis. These can be summarised as follows:

1. Create consistency – based on long term strategy of continuing to trade and provide work for employees.

2. Adopt a new philosophy of accepting leadership responsibility for change.

3. Do not rely on inspection for quality management – instead build quality into the process – it is better to get it right first time than rely on capturing errors and correcting afterwards.

4. Aim for long term trust with suppliers – based on minimising overall costs rather than holding them to lowest price.

5. Constantly improve to reduce costs and improve quality.

6. Provide on-the-job training and apprenticeships.

7. Supervise to lead rather than control.

8. Remove fear from the workplace.

9. Break down departmental barriers. The silo approach causes unhealthy internal competition and loses focus from the ultimate customer.

10. Eliminate slogans.
11. Remove work floor targets that discourage pride in workmanship.
12. Remove management targets that discourage pride in workmanship.
13. Institute programmes for self-improvement and development.
14. Seek commitment from all for transformation of the organisation.

Kaizen – continuous improvement

Kaizen is about striving for continuous incremental improvement. The converse is 'kaikaku' which means revolutionary radical improvement. The approach is cyclical, as once completed it is started again. Each turn of the cycle should be a refinement on the last so that we incrementally move towards perfection.

The success of a kaizen continuous improvement programme depends largely on the culture of the organisation. For Kaizen to work effectively, this culture should be based upon:

1. Ethics	demonstrating by company codes and behaviours what the customer perceives to be right.
2. Integrity	based on openness and honesty. The loss of integrity can have a significant impact on customers in the information age (e.g. adverse media stories about tax liabilities).

3. Trust	is established from ethics and integrity, it is vital in order for TQM efforts to achieve their objectives and encourage commitment from customers and employees.
4. Training	ongoing improvement requires new employees to understand and adopt processes, and existing employees to be updated on new processes and other changes.
5. Teamwork	a healthy team ethos will ensure consistency and produce creative thinking from improving processes.
6. Leadership	without the visible commitment, enthusiasm and clearly communicated vision of the leadership it will be extremely difficult, if not impossible, to achieve TQM in the workplace.
7. Communication	clear unambiguous communication encourages consolidation of TQM achievements and progress for continuous improvement.
8. Recognition	Recognition of teams and individuals encourages the development of further suggestions for improvements and commitment to the organisation.

PDCA (Deming) change cycle

The lean change process can be illustrated by the PDCA or kaizen cycle for continuous improvement. The same steps could be used for any change (including kaikaku). The difference is that for kaizen/continuous improvement, the cycle never stops but merely repeats itself.

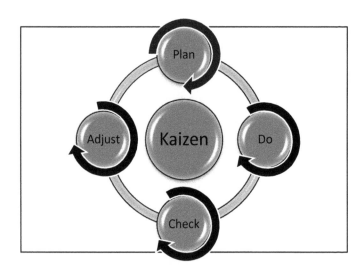

Figure 8: PDCA cycle adapted for kaizen

Plan – this involves scoping and agreeing the objectives to be covered, including agreeing any metrics to measure the achievement of the change. A plan should cover the Who? Why? How? When? questions and arrangements to gather metrics to measure the progress of the change.

Do – carry out the plan to make the change, collect metrics on its effectiveness and lessons learnt for future changes.

Change (sometimes referred to as study) – complete analysis of the metrics and other data (e.g. surveys of prospective customers). The results should be compared to the predictions made in the original plan. This can also include testing and show and tells, etc.

Adjust (aka 'Act') – implement the change and decide what is to be covered in the next iteration cycle.

Kaikaku

Sometimes organisations require large radical changes – rather than slower evolutionary ones. This could be in response to a 'PEST' change (political, economic, social and technological) or after, for example, a major business change, such as a merger or acquisition. Most traditional projects are generally based on kaikaku. Lean projects are based on kaizen (gradual change) and are therefore more aligned with business as usual activity than with projects and programmes. A number of books on lean just ignore kaikaku completely. In *Lean Thinking,* however, Womack and Jones recommend a combination; using kaikaku to make the large changes and then kaizen to make the smaller ongoing incremental changes. The implementation of lean thinking itself may require a kaikaku type approach to radically change the culture, tools and approach of the organisation. It can be used to reach an initial benchmark that can then be further improved with the use of kaizen. The skill for management is to know which approach should be used in each situation – the rapid major implementation (via kaikaku) or the sustained longer improvement of kaizen? Both will use lean tools and techniques – the difference is the scope and timespan of each.

If we take the concept of kaizen, rather than kaikaku, to a logical conclusion we could be seeing the end of large scale projects and a move to constantly changing processes. This would require a radical re-think about how we perform, manage and govern projects.

The 5Ss

Lean thinking has a tool to help with housekeeping, and as we will see, this tool has wider uses. It is called the 5Ss. I am always puzzled how alliteration works in both Japanese and English – but maybe something gets lost in translation. Like most of lean, the approach is thought to have started at Toyota. The five Ss are:

1. Seiri (translated as sort or simplify)
2. Seiton (set, stabilise, orderliness or organise)
3. Seiso (shine)
4. Seiketsu (standardise)
5. Shitsuke (sustain).

Seiri (translated as sort or simplify)

Seiri is the identification and implementation of the most successful organisation of the workspace. It involves the identification of what is required, when it is required, and by whom. By implication this includes removing clutter, or those things not required, as they will cause confusion and potential waste, as well as being potential hazards. This can include the reduction of work in progress and removal of excess materials. One local authority was spending far higher than average amounts on office stationery. We conducted a simple audit to review the levels of paper, pencils, pens, etc. by walking around all of the offices and looking in stationery cupboards. We found that there were many years of supplies being hoarded and not used – including gallons of correcting fluid that was past its use by date. By tagging and recording items for disposal or return to central store, we were able to identify what really needed to be bought and what could be returned to central store for re-issue instead of buying new supplies.

In the 1990s we found six sacks of town gas valves (used before the introduction of North Sea Gas in the 1970s) at a local authority housing depot that were of no use. They were constantly getting in the way of staff and being moved or transferred between depots. By flagging them they were eventually sold for scrap.

Such reviews are now common throughout the public and private sectors to identify potential clutter and waste. Other examples include the organisation of operating theatre trays, or storage of medical records in the NHS.

In summary, seiri is about reviewing the workspace to ensure that it is organised to reduce wasted effort and is clear of items that are not likely to be required for the task in hand.

Seiton (set, stabilise, orderliness or organise)

Having reviewed the workspace (seiri – above), the next step is to implement improvements. To coin a phrase, seiton is about 'a place for everything and everything in its place'. It is also about ensuring the right quantities are stored in the right places.

I once met an IT operations manager who told me whenever he was called in to solve a problem, the first thing he always did was to tidy the working area. His philosophy was that it is easier to solve problems in a clean and tidy environment. It is easier to be productive in an uncluttered, tidy work area. Ask any experienced and skilled craftsman and they will agree. The impact is not only physical cleanliness – it also has a psychological impact on most of us, making us feel happier and safer, and the implication is that we are prepared to work harder and more carefully.

These days this is as true of the virtual workspace as it is of the physical workspace. I have worked with people who regularly have over 500 unread emails in their inbox – and usually have not noticed the important ones that I have sent to them.

Professional craftsman, for example, take great effort to organise their tools and other requirements, and to ensure the working area is well organised so that they:

- Know the items they need most are close at hand.
- Know the location of all their tools and can quickly tell if one is missing, or in need of repair.
- Can ensure tools are cleaned and maintained after use.

- Avoid injury from badly stored blades or other potentially dangerous tools.
- Know what additional tools they need to buy and do not buy tools they already have.
- Reduce continuous moving, recording and storing of items no longer needed.

Another example could be the way that modern kitchens are organised to ensure that the tools or ingredients needed most (e.g. chopping boards and knives) are close to hand, whilst those needed less often are stored out of the way (e.g. ice cream makers in the winter or Christmas cake decorations for most of the year).

This can extend to computer desktops – for example in the way that applications are organised, ensuring that users only open those required. Emphasis is on reducing clutter to make the workspace easier and more effective to use.

In summary, seiton is about ensuring a standard way of doing things, as supported by an organised workspace. This includes organisation of requirements to ensure they can be found and used with minimal effort and waste.

Seiso (shine, sweep or clean)

Most of us prefer to work, live and shop in clean and tidy environments. These are also safer, more secure and more efficient than the alternate. This is why most offices have a clear desk policy and insist that meeting rooms are cleared after each meeting. I wouldn't want to take a prospective client into a meeting room with dirty coffee cups and whiteboards showing confidential information about other customers – it would definitely lead to a negative perception.

Although most of us like to be in a clean environment, most of us also do not like to actually do anything to make it clean. I like the sign in my local chip shop 'Don't lean – Clean'. It shows an emphasis on hygiene and also makes individual staff responsible for ensuring a clean environment. The implementation of seiso is based upon:

- removing potential sources of contamination
- regular inspections and feedback
- clearly assigned responsibilities for cleanliness of specific areas
- schedules to show who does what and when
- preparation – ensuring the tools and materials are to hand (see seiton above).

We even have this at our local bowls club – I know what dates I am on cleaning duty and there is a checklist to ensure I know what I need to do, and telling me where I can find the vacuum and the dusters.

In summary, a clean workspace is safer and healthier, it promotes customer confidence and is more efficient as it reduces waste and supports standardisation.

Seiketsu (standardise, embed process)

Seiketsu is the means for sustaining the first three Ss as described above. Drives to improve housekeeping can be seen in some organisations as one-offs or just 'flavour of the month' topics. In which case they become forgotten during the next management initiative and so need to be repeated at regular intervals to achieve the same status quo with little progress forward. Seiketsu is about embedding processes for seiri, seiton and seiso so they become part of normal everyday routines rather than being one off exercises. This includes scheduling 5S tasks and ensuring that the infrastructure and other resources are in place, including independent audit, to support the related activities. This is important to indicate early any falling in standards that may not be apparent to those performing the processes.

The benefits of this standardisation are that it provides a schedule of 5S activities, embeds the habits for the first three Ss, and begins problem solving whilst promoting discipline and the ability to sustain activities.

Shitsuke (sustain)

The fifth S is about discipline and retaining the benefits achieved. Whereas Seiketsu (the fourth S) is about introducing formal rigorous reviews, shitsuke is less mechanical and more about approaches to change behaviours in the medium to longer term. It is hence about persuasion and stimulation and so is based on:

- Communication of the objectives and building of trust so that processes and procedures become the habitual norm.
- Acceptance by all.
- Awareness of what concepts they need to understand and the techniques to be used. This includes new joiners.

- Reward and recognition for effort so that the benefits are shared and buy-in is obtained.
- Time to complete the assigned activities.
- Structure – What? Who? When? How? performed and how recorded.

By creating the right behaviours, we establish and maintain more efficient, safer and more secure workplaces. This not only includes the physical workplace but also cyberspace – for example by encouraging best password and other IT security practices.

Auditing TQM the change process (kaikaku and kaizen)

The audit of the change process will vary depending on the circumstances. The following guideline questions are intended to provide a generic approach. One of the best sources for audit of TQM and PDCA is the ISO9001/19011 standard. The 'check' stage of PDCA could itself be considered as audit. The ISO website states:

> ISO19011:2011 provides guidance on auditing management systems, including the principles of auditing, managing an audit programme and conducting management system audits, as well as guidance on the evaluation of competence of individuals involved in the audit process, including the person managing the audit programme, auditors and audit teams.

Any audit of TQM needs to first consider the arrangements and culture that management has established to achieve TQM. This can then be used as the benchmark for individual project or assignment audits. The following table summarises some of the areas to consider:

Ethics/integrity/trust

- How has the code of ethics been updated and communicated to all?
- What is the evidence that it is understood and applied consistently and effectively?
- Is there evidence in the press and social media that demonstrates an apparent lack of integrity? If so, how have management reacted to this?
- Is there evidence from staff and customer surveys that they trust the organisation?
- Are there adequate signs of commitment of TQM?

Training/teamwork/leadership/recognition/communication

- What training do new joiners receive to make them aware of the organisation's commitment to TQM and codes of conduct, etc. (obtain and review copies)?
- Is there a culture for celebrating and sharing success?

The best way to audit the 5Ss is by direct observation. You can often tell an organisation's attitude to order and cleanliness just from the reception area.

Seiri (translated as sort or simplify)

1. What policies and procedures are in place for archiving and retention?
2. How often are stock levels reviewed to identify items no longer required?

3. What evidence is there to show that the policies and procedures are being applied effectively in practice (e.g. no evidence of clutter)?

Seiton (set, stabilise, orderliness or organise)

4. Are team sites and work areas well structured and organised?
5. What suggestions do the team have for improving the organisation of these?

Seiso (shine)

6. Are there any signs of contamination?
7. What evidence is there to show that policies for cleaning and sorting are applied in everyday practice?

Seiketsu (standardise)

8. What evidence is there to confirm that audits and review inspections are conducted regularly and that findings (positive and negative) are reported back to the teams concerned?

Shitsuke (sustain)

9. How are benefits achieved, quantified and staff recognised and rewarded for their efforts?

This area may also be suitable for softer controls, such as interviewing key staff to understand their motivation and attitudes and how these align with the expected ethos, etc. that the organisation is trying to achieve.

Summary

The pursuit of perfection is a key principle of lean. This pursuit may be a radical change (kaikaku) or by continuous improvement (kaizen). Both should be underpinned by a strong commitment to total quality management.

Audit/checking has an important role to ensure that continuous improvement is being achieved. The use of the 5Ss also demonstrates that this commitment includes the provision and maintenance of a workplace that will encourage continuous improvement.

CHAPTER 8: LEAN SOFTWARE DEVELOPMENT

Overview

Traditional methods of developing computer software, both in house/bespoke and in the form of commercially available packages, have not always been fully effective. There are countless stories of systems that do not work, packages full of features with limited actual benefit, implementation delays, new releases that don't work effectively and cost overruns. Nor can these traditional methods keep up with constant developments in hardware and other technologies. What is needed is an approach that reduces waste, is able to provide what customer's value, and can be continuously improved. Sound familiar? Yes, that's why a number of organisations are now using lean and agile methodologies to improve their software acquisition and development.

The term 'lean software development' is attributed to Mary and Tom Poppendieck from their book *Lean Software Development*. The book proposes seven principles of lean software development, very like the lean principles:

1. Eliminate waste
2. Build quality in
3. Create knowledge
4. Defer commitment
5. Deliver fast

6. Respect people
7. Optimise the whole.

Each of the above are achieved by using standard lean tools described elsewhere in this book. In this chapter we will consider each of the lean software development principles and how they can be audited.

Eliminate waste

In lean, waste is anything that does not add customer value (muda). Waste can be in the process of creating the software or in the software that is produced – causing issues for future customers/users. For software, muda can take many forms, including:

- incomplete code or features
- additional manual processes required to ensure operation, control or compliance of the solution
- features that do not add benefit (e.g. how much of the functionality of your spreadsheet tool do you actually use?)
- burdensome workflows
- waiting time during transactions
- motion – for example calls to other systems
- features, or even whole systems, abandoned before they are completed and delivered.

The first requirement is to identify all waste in the development cycle, i.e. anything that does not add customer value. Waste can be caused by over-bureaucratic project management processes that do not mitigate any risk, or production of features not needed. Defects are also wasteful as they can cause error and take time and effort to find and eradicate. Scope creep and churn are other causes of waste – leading to unnecessary features to be developed, tested and rolled out, causing an operating overhead and possibly impacting completion of features that are actually needed.

One reason for this waste, is that we set unrealistic expectations for users – asking them to blue sky think what they want and then trying to develop that in a single pass (a waterfall approach), rather than providing prototypes of minimum viable product and then incrementally building enhancements on that (an agile approach).

Value stream mapping and strong challenge processes can be used to minimise development waste and focus on real customer value. These should focus on real business benefit value, rather than nice to have features.

Build quality in

As we saw for manufacturing, quality can be achieved either by getting it right first time – building quality into the product and process (a preventative control), or by inspection and correction after the event (a detective control). Traditional development has been based on a build-test-rectify-re-test process. Often the testing step is restricted in time, with insufficient time for rectification and re-testing if faults are found. Hence frequently implementation is delayed, possibly because of faults that only impact a minor part of the release. Getting it right first time is cheaper and more effective – as there is better learning for future projects, and the need for tracking defects, rectification/re-testing is vastly reduced.

The use of lean agile techniques, such as test driven development, whereby testing is performed as the code is written and the program code is then changed immediately, reduce these areas of waste. This moves testing away from a detective control to find defects, to a preventative control to reduce defects occurring. Some testing and verification is still necessary to provide overall assurance that the software is fit for purpose and adds the value the customer wants.

Create knowledge (aka amplify learning)

Traditional waterfall projects assume that all requirements are known and can be designed and communicated prior to the writing of any code. I have been frequently frustrated when writing requirements and design – no matter how detailed I am there are also questions – or worse still incorrect assumptions made by the developer. Also, I may be asking for a feature to be written in a particular way and there is a better, often cheaper way of providing the same functionality I am unaware of. My knowledge is incomplete – as is that of the developer, and the use of the written word to communicate, complete with re-draftings and approvals, is time consuming and wasteful. A far more 'agile' approach is by working together to provide a high-level requirement and then developing this by proto-typing/testing and demonstration and discussion. This approach also gives more flexibility if the stakeholders change their minds about what needs to be developed to add value. The knowledge to develop the software is hence created in a more dynamic and flexible way than the traditional process that heavily relies upon documentation.

As human beings we learn from our mistakes. Software development is no exception.

This lack of documentation can present us, as auditors, with challenges – we would much rather have a nice list of detailed requirements we can tick off against. However, with imagination and better interaction with developers and stakeholders, we can still ensure that the software is being developed economically, efficiently and effectively and that all necessary control and governance requirements have been included.

The use of short iteration cycles in lean/agile speeds the learning processes and reduces the level of impact defects will have. By working together, there is a synergistic benefit as the developers and business representatives learn about any issues together and can find a mutually acceptable solution.

Defer commitment (aka decide as late as possible)

As a firefighter, my father was trained to deal with life-threatening, quickly changing situations. Part of that training involved making sure that they had all available information before making a decision. It's no good rushing into a burning building, with no-one inside, to put water on chemicals that will react violently with the water, for example.

The Poppendieck's suggest applying the same approach to software development. Irreversible decisions should be taken as late as possible, so they can be based on more up-to-date information, often facts rather than assumptions, and the knowledge gained from the development so far. Whilst less risky decisions should be made as soon as they are required, some decisions made early in the process may cause issues later on, as the options available for the later decision have been inadvertently restricted. Planning can still be undertaken, based on different assumptions and options rather than commitments.

Deliver fast

We live in an age that seeks immediate gratification. When I was at school, if I wanted to order a book it would take two weeks to arrive and I had to collect it from the local store. Now I can have it delivered by post the next day, or within minutes if I want the e-book format.

If I have a problem in the office I want it fixed NOW – not (and then only potentially) in two years' time when a new system is implemented with loads of other stuff that I am not interested in using. During that two years I will change my mind a number of times about what I want and how it should be provided. Give me what I need now, and the rest of the features can wait until I need them. I want rapid delivery of a quality product. That's my Wow factor.

Just in time production can be applied to software. When responding to changes in legislation or regulation it often is. Speed also reduces waste – there is less chance for expensive changes and work is focused on the 'must have' requirements. This speed also allows experimentation and creative thinking – key components of problem solving.

Respect people (aka empower the team)

I once worked with someone who said the problem with their organisation was that it 'recruited eagles and treated them like turkeys'. Respect was based on years of experience, and in some cases the Old (school) Boys network. Everyone's view should be respected in a team – regardless of their job grade or pay cheque. In agile, the aim is for teams to be self-organising. This has the benefit of enabling all in the team to use and share the experience and knowledge they may have gained elsewhere.

Good managers lead by listening and advising – not by dictating the solution. I once heard a celebrity chef say on television that a good leader 'tells people what to do, lets them get on with it, and then just checks when they have done it'. This is quite different to the approach of some of his famous contemporaries who lead by swearing and fear. The difference is that his staff are loyal to him over a longer period of time. We need to trust people to make their own mistakes, in a safe environment, and then learn from them.

One phrase I find very disrespectful is when I am referred to as a resource – to be managed by human resources. I am a man not a number! I need to be motivated and respected by my co-workers. To achieve this, I may need to speak directly to key stakeholders and I need to be sure that I can rely on my supervisor to support me in difficult times. In return I offer the same for those who work with me.

Optimise the whole (aka see the whole)

For software development to be effective – even if just a line of code – it needs to be seen in the context of the wider issue. A small change in one program can have a dramatic effect elsewhere in the system. Interactions are as important as individual sets of program code. For example, a change in a user table may cause a completely different effect when the new code is introduced. It is also important to ensure that any fix solves the real problem – the root cause rather than just a symptom. The fishbone or 5 Whys technique can help to achieve this.

Audit of lean software development

When auditing or providing assurance for lean software developments, many of the audit considerations in the previous chapters will still apply. The reviewer should also consider the normal software considerations, such as security and the adequacy of testing, governance and adequacy of documentation.

In addition, you could consider:

- How the project plan ensures the seven areas are covered during project development.
- How the final product demonstrates that the development process has considered the seven areas.

Summary

Lean thinking can be applied to software development – the key is to consider the underlying principles of lean rather than focusing on individual practices and tools.

CHAPTER 9: GOVERNANCE OF LEAN PROJECTS

Overview

The Association for Project Management (APM) defines governance as follows:

> '... the set of policies, regulations, functions, processes, procedures and responsibilities that define the establishment, management and control of projects ...'
> (see http://knowledge.apm.org.uk/bok/governance)

From this we can see that governance is about control – i.e. the reduction or management of risk. It also involves stated principles, processes, clearly defined roles and responsibilities, and some ongoing independent review or audit. We will consider each of these themes in this chapter, together with the challenge of maintaining security, governance and control, whilst at the same time reducing waste and delivering what customers want.

Lean projects and activities also require governance to demonstrate how risks have been identified, monitored and controlled.

Governance risks for lean

PRINCE2 defines a risk as:

> 'An uncertain event or set of events that, should it occur, will have an effect on the achievement of the objectives.'

We measure risk by assigning a likelihood or probability that it will occur and a potential impact if it does.

Like all projects, the main risks could lead to issues associated with:

- cost overruns
- time overruns
- failure to meet agreed objectives (including controls and expected quality levels).

Also, given the experimental and changing nature of lean projects, there is a higher risk from unknown/difficult to predict issues.

Individual risks can be expressed in terms of an event, trigger and consequence. For example:

> The lean project may be delayed (event) because the main sponsor leaves (trigger), resulting in failure to achieve predicted savings in the medium term (consequence).

> Additional costs may be incurred, because the main supplier takes legal action to delay early closure of the contract, leading to delays in achieving savings and bad publicity.

There are a number of techniques to identify and assess risks for a lean project:

1. Review of the strategic risks of the organisation to identify those relevant to the project (e.g. relating to competitor activity, compliance, cost constraints).
2. Workshops with project representatives and senior stakeholders to brainstorm likely risk areas, to create risk heat maps and suggest mitigations.

3. Review of lessons learnt from previous similar projects, including the ability to realise benefits from similar projects, causes of delays or cost overruns.

4. The maturity of the organisation in undertaking this type of project.

5. SWOT analysis (strengths, weaknesses, opportunities and threats).

6. Root cause analysis to ensure that the underlying cause of a risk is documented and assessed rather than just a symptom or consequence.

Once the risks have been identified and assessed they should be logged and recorded so that governance reporting can show how they are being mitigated, whether new risks arise, and to show where the risk results in an actual issue.

Governance principles and organisation

The stated principles (in the form of guidelines, standards and procedures), an organisational structure, and culture of an organisation, will set the context for the way that governance operates. They help to communicate the level of empowerment and authority within the organisation. In particular, how the strategic objectives set by senior management and the Board are translated into operational and tactical management at other levels.

Lean governance is based more on delegation and enabling teams so they are motivated to achieve their required objectives for their projects or other areas of responsibility. This is different to the more traditional approach on projects based upon centralised command and control, with project management offices and steering boards often providing very detailed levels of control, dictating standardised reporting and ways of working, and defining priorities sometimes to quite a low level of detail. Agile and lean encourage greater autonomy within teams. For example, in Agile Scrum each team will often set its own charter defining the working 'rules' for the team. It is based on the principle that teams are composed of mature professionals.

I once worked for an organisation where there was a moratorium on leave in January and February each year as these were busy months. But our team's busy period was May and June. So we could book as much leave as we wanted in June but not in January! Lean recognises the need for flexibility. It is not only in the interests of the team but of the organisation and its customers.

This requires a pragmatic approach from those responsible for governance in an organisation. This relinquishing of control can make them feel uncomfortable and insecure, and the risk is that as soon as something goes wrong they will revert to a more traditional command and control structure. Given the experimental nature of lean, there is an increased likelihood of such events. However, a good, pragmatic, lean governing body will be aware of this and take steps to:

1. Ensure the impact is minimalised, for example by use of pilot projects and planned release based on risk.
2. Have a contingency plan to consider how they will react in certain situations.
3. Clearly state the reasons for the rules they set, rather than just stating that they should be followed.

4. Create an empowered environment where people are aware of the risks they can take and any limitations.

5. Ensure that everyone has the resources required to deliver what is expected of them, on budget and on time. For example, this may mean the provision of tools and processes that are non-standard for an organisation but will allow better interaction with third parties or collaborative working within the team.

6. Be supportive, providing recognition for achievements and support, rather than apportionment of blame and recrimination when things go wrong.

The above will demonstrate that the Board are aiming for high-level strategic governance rather than detailed micro-management. These steps should be communicated and affirmed by visible actions and behaviours. Where teams know they are trusted and have some control over how they manage themselves, they are less likely to ignore and rebel against the rules. Governance then becomes embedded in the process, rather than being seen as a wasteful muda overhead.

Imagine a scenario where a lean project has delivered the expected small benefits and now could be expanded across the whole organisation, with a very high return for low cost. This should not be a problem – you would expect most organisations to say 'go ahead, get on with it'. However, in my experience a number of organisations have such rigid controls over projects that the roll out would be stopped, as there is not the budget to pay for it – the budget is already committed to other projects, some of which may have a lower forecasted rate of return. One organisation I know of expects a return on investment within one year, even though they capitalise project expenditure over three years.

A lean organisation has a more customer driven approach to project pipeline management. For example, by providing a fast track for projects that can demonstrate immediate strategic benefits. This will be based on a scorecard system to demonstrate the value to the customer.

Governance processes and metrics

Good governance relies on a framework of processes and metrics to enable informed decisions to be made. The main practices associated with lean hence have an impact on how governance is achieved and monitored. Especially:

- The use of delivery in smaller iterations.
- Flexible milestones relating to risk and benefit rather than pre-determined stage gates.
- The project approach itself changing based on learnings as the work progresses to achieve continuous learning.
- Compliance and control embedded into the process, rather than added on as an afterthought.
- Focusing on the best metrics, rather than ones that encourage the wrong behaviours.

The use of delivery within specified shorter time boxes needs quicker and slicker decision making. In a time box of 28 days, if an issue arises it needs to be resolved immediately – it is no good deferring to the next steering board which may be in two months' time. Also, if the new process is to be released within the next 30 days, the mind is more focused than it is two years away. Governance needs to consider the implications of this – also the impact of team fatigue, when in effect you can have a go live every 28 days. The release procedures of some organisations may be too inflexible to allow the releases to happen at the optimal time for the lean or agile project, causing delays in achieving identified benefits and a risk that competitors may get there first.

The pressure to make a release can, however, be a risk itself. There still needs to be go/no go type decision taken independently so that all of the potential risks are identified and resolved. This could be based on leaner testing and more emphasis on customer value – for example the product or service may meet the requirements (MVP – or minimum viable product) but will it fully meet the customers' expectations for look and feel (MLP – minimum loveable product)? This could be just as important to the success of the product with customers or other users.

I worked on a hybrid agile/lean/waterfall project where we demonstrated the application to senior management prior to release. They agreed that we had met the brief but asked for some refinements to make it more easy to use and with a more attractive user interface. Go live was put back by about one month whilst we made these changes. Those from a waterfall background considered this as a failure. Those of us from a more agile mindset, however, considered this to be a success. The final version was improved and customer feedback was very encouraging.

The real metric of importance was not around time to release – it was about whether customers could and would use the tool and have an enjoyable experience in the process. We also developed specific KPIs to monitor the process post go live, to identify any potential issues. These were just temporary metrics and in the longer term different metrics were required.

Project approaches used need to be adaptable to fit the nature of a lean project. Every project is different with different risks, compliance and security requirements, team members and extent of agility/lean required. However, most organisations stick with a fixed, rigid style of governance – this can cause a tremendous overhead on smaller iteration projects, offsetting some of the achieved benefits. Greater flexibility can provide improved team productivity, leading to a more efficient, effective and economic process – with better continuous learning and improvement. This is also more rewarding for the teams concerned, especially where they can see their suggestions and comments being acted upon promptly, which was not always the case on 'lessons learnt' sessions for waterfall projects I have attended in the past.

By embedding or automating lean governance, it becomes easier to comply than to not comply! If, however, the effort required is large, teams will consider it as waste and focus instead on what they see as being more important. This could become a risk, particularly if there are regulatory or reporting requirements (e.g. for compliance with Sarbanes-Oxley Act), as these views may not be those of the senior stakeholders. Some human judgement will still be required but often lean principles can be applied to simplify and automate the process for data gathering, wherever possible using metrics and tools that the team use for their management to summarise key points for upward reporting. Getting governance/ compliance right first time is surely a lean principle worth adhering to – reducing waste later in the process or elsewhere in the organisation.

To achieve this, metrics need to be relevant and simple to obtain, especially as lean projects are likely to be subject to continuous monitoring, as the regular cycles may be too long to identify any issues during the life of the shorter project. To be relevant, lean metrics need to be related to the key drivers of waste and customer benefit. The lean project should be run in a lean way. There needs to be some way of taking the management metrics for the project and converting them into the governance metrics required by the organisation. Data for metrics should be accurate, timely, consistent over reporting periods, and capable of being repeatable – i.e. results over different projects will be compatible with similar assumptions and timelines.

Governance responsibilities and roles

Policies, processes and measures are important components of governance. However, to be fully effective governance also requires commitment from people. As a contractor, I have worked in many organisations and they all start with a health and safety induction. All of these emphasise values, such as ensuring everyone gets home safely and speaking up. Yet my attitude in a risk situation will depend more on the culture and my feelings than it will on checklists and procedures. Indeed, some say that the procedures go too far (phrases, such as 'health and safety gone mad'). So policies, such as not taking phone calls whilst driving, or what to do when the fire alarm goes, are important – but more important is 'do I feel empowered to challenge when I see these policies being broken'? Am I able to challenge the individual and make them aware of the risks they are taking? This depends on the culture of the organisation and its attitude to risk. The same principles apply to lean project teams and how empowered they feel they are. Good lean governance relies on this feeling of empowerment, as underpinned by promotion of self-organising teams and the alignment of policies to lean values.

The term self-organising is often confused with self-managing teams. The lean project team is still part of the organisation – there to provide value to customers and reduce waste. Self-organisation in a lean context means lean teams/individuals have greater control over:

- The work performed – however this selection needs to be within the strategic framework and priorities of the organisation.
- How they commit to and perform work, including just in time planning.
- The application of the 5Ss.

The team leaders are still accountable and need to ensure adequate communication of the plan, progress, risks and issues, both within the team and to senior stakeholders.

The alignment of HR policies to lean objectives is to ensure that people are treated as mature professionals, and talent is retained and motivated to be innovative as well as productive. Some organisations seem to stifle innovation – it is a greater risk to someone's career to try a new idea that partly fails than to not make the suggestion in the first place. Innovative organisations I have worked in take a different approach – making it acceptable to fail, as even if the first three out of four ideas fail, the fourth may be a cracker!

Arrangements for personal development, performance measurement and reward need to reflect the desire for collaboration and team working. For example, the contribution of a good mentor can be more effective in ensuring customer value and reducing waste than the direct benefit achieved from a single individual's delivery. One way to measure this is to place greater importance on $360°$ feedback from peers rather than just relying on feedback from often remote management. The emphasis should be on encouraging the innovative/entrepreneurial behaviours required to drive customer value and reduce waste.

In 1968 Melvin Conway submitted a paper 'How Do Committees Invent?' to *Datamation*, the major IT magazine at that time. The basis has become known as Conway's Law and can be summarised as follows:

> 'Any organization that designs a system …. will produce a design whose structure is a copy of the organisation's communication structure.'[2]

To put it another way, innovative solutions require innovative organisations and governance. I cannot imagine Facebook being created from within an

---

[2] Source *www.melconway.com/Home/Conways_Law.html*

organisation, such as the large computer companies in the 1970s, or in a government department. Likewise, modern developers may struggle to create the highly defined, structured and compliant software often associated with these organisations.

Lean also relies on quality – and this too needs to be embedded within the team ethos and HR policies. But it needs to be defined in a lean way – quality is often taken as being about ticking the right boxes, however as we have seen, lean puts the emphasis on customer value and so it is this that is the real measure. I have been in call centres when all of a sudden there is a loud whoop of joy and round of applause. This is because one of the operators has received a perfect score on the customer feedback process – this leads to instant recognition and reward. For project teams this is rare. On some projects the team has been rewarded with anything from doughnuts to a team night out. On other projects, however, despite the success of the project there were insufficient funds to fund such a reward.

Challenge of maintaining security and control whilst reducing waste

Governance is still necessary for lean projects but it needs to be seen in a context of encouraging the right behaviours and coming from the team up, rather than being dictated as a series of restrictive policies dictated from the top.

There can be a trade-off between control and the need to be lean. For example, a review may identify an area as potential muda which actually has an indirect impact on governance or compliance across the organisation, or on the ability of the organisation to maintain reasonable levels of IT security. I have also come across the converse though where control was increased following a lean change. In this case, monthly reporting activities had been transferred to a centralised offshore team. There was supposed to be a significant saving, however, this was not realised as the onshore teams continued to do some of the control activities, duplicating what was being done offshore. The monitoring of controls had not been updated to reflect the current process.

Audits of lean governance

An independent audit of a lean project or assurance exercise will ensure that:

- The governance process is appropriate for the project.
- Benefits obtained are real and are directly attributable to the project.
- Monitoring is in place to identify any small changes required to the process, etc. to eliminate any additional waste.
- There is sufficient visibility of the importance of the project.
- Stakeholders can be given independent assurance on the effectiveness, economy and efficiency of the project process and assurance that any issues discovered will be avoided in future projects.

The following questions could be included in a review of lean project governance:

1. Have the governing body the right level of control over the governance of the project, without too much involvement in day-to-day project management?

2. Are all team members aware of their governance responsibilities?

3. Is there evidence of ongoing monitoring and review throughout the life of the project?

4. How can it be demonstrated that the project has met its objectives and achieved the benefits?

5. What steps (e.g. independent review) have been take to identify any additional benefits?

Summary

The governance of lean projects and other lean activities is important to ensure that key stakeholders have the comfort and assurance that their key objectives will be achieved. It is also important to ensure that there is ongoing activity to maintain continuous improvement, and to identify and communicate areas of best practice (and areas for development).

CHAPTER 10: USING LEAN APPROACHES FOR YOUR LEAN PROJECT AUDIT/REVIEW

Introduction

The use of lean thinking techniques to deliver internal and external audits, or assurance reviews of lean projects, has a number of advantages including:

1. Leading by example.
2. Providing a learning environment and a test bed for auditors to try out lean thinking.
3. Focusing on real stakeholder needs.
4. Becoming more commercial by focusing on what is important to the end customer.
5. Getting to the root causes of issues, rather than making recommendations that merely fix a symptom of the problem.
6. Reducing wasteful audits and reporting and thereby reducing costs.
7. Becoming more effective in providing compliance, whilst also highlighting issues that may reduce costs and improve customer service for the area under review.

Some organisations, I am sure, see audit as a necessary evil – an inconvenience and cost overhead (or worse a muda). To a certain extent, some traditional audit teams have not done much to break this image. However, this is now changing and many audit teams have been adopting lean thinking – some without even realising it.

10: Using Lean Approaches for Your Lean Project Audit/Review

In this chapter we will consider how lean thinking can be applied to audit or assurance review. Throughout this chapter I have referred to 'the auditor', however, the same principles apply to anyone performing an assurance review of a lean project or other activity.

Identifying audit customers

Why do we do audits or assurance reviews? All audits are to provide some form of independent comfort that there is proper governance and compliance, and advice on how to improve. However, there is an opportunity for auditors to provide so much more. Internal auditors often have an overview of the organisation that is not available to many in an organisation. Because they consider a number of different areas, there is the opportunity to share best practice and lessons learnt from previous reviews in a different area of the business. This is one reason why many organisations see internal audit as an important part of career development for their high-flying trainees.

One of the accolades I most enjoy when auditing is when someone says 'that's a good question' – it shows that I have led the auditee to look at the issue from a different angle.

During the review of the 2009 banking crisis, the House of Lords and others looked at the role of internal audit. The concern was that they were too focused on the needs of immediate management, in some cases to the point where they were not considering the real risks, rather than considering the needs of the wider 'customer' base.

So who are the customers of the review/audit? By considering the wider group, it helps to ensure the audit is providing a better service – customers include:

- the immediate auditee and their managers/senior management
- the Board – especially the audit committee
- regulators
- shareholders/other financers
- business partners of the organisation
- customers of the organisation.

I have listed the above in the order that they are normally considered by auditors. At first it seems strange to include end customers in the list. But they are the ones ultimately paying for the audit – therefore they should gain some benefit. Also, if an organisation is moving to lean thinking, placing more emphasis on customer value, it is important that their requirements are considered. For example, does the audit function generate more savings (including risk reduction) than it costs to operate?

Adding real value

The phrase 'I am your auditor and I am here to help you' is always an amusing one – and one often not believed by auditees. However, there are opportunities for auditors to add benefit, without losing their independence or objectivity.

As a Board member on audit committees, I have always found it most useful adding real value when we have meetings with the auditors without management being present. This 'off the record' briefing gives an opportunity to discuss issues which the auditor, especially if an external provider, may not be willing to share in a formal report. It is also a good opportunity for the audit committee to make clear what their expectations are. For example, before the commencement of any audit I would expect the auditors to have informal discussions with the main stakeholders. As with any meetings with customers, the auditors may need to limit expectations if the requirements are unrealistic but it is better to be clear on this in the scoping documents so there can be no misunderstandings as to what is to be delivered.

The audit process for reviewing a lean project is similar to any assurance or audit review and can be summarised as:

* plan and scope
* listen and review
* gather and review corroborative evidence
* publish findings and recommendations.

The Institute of Internal Auditor's Publication, *Internal Auditing: Adding Value across the Board*, describes internal audit as:

> 'An independent, objective, assurance and consulting activity that adds value to and improves an organisation's operations.'[3]

This definition covers the consulting role that internal audit often provides, in addition to the compliance role.

---

[3] Source *https://na.theiia.org/about-ia/PublicDocuments/Internal_Auditing-Adding_Value_Across_the_Board.pdf*

The implementation of Sarbanes-Oxley (SOX) gives a good illustration of how auditors can apply lean thinking to all that they do. Most impacted audit teams reviewed the quality of the design and operation of the financial reporting controls needed for SOX compliance. The better ones went beyond that to identify:

- Where there was wastage due to over or duplicated control.
- How the same level of control could be achieved using alternate controls (e.g. through centralisation or automation).
- Controls where their risk level is well below the cost of the control.

This could be achieved without impacting independence or the quality of the audit opinion on the adequacy of the control framework. One organisation I worked with estimated that each SOX control cost about $1,000 per year to maintain and test. So any reduction in the number of controls can have a large saving in reducing waste – far greater than the cost of the audit.

Identifying and mapping the audit value stream

Good planning of the review should ensure that the process for the review has been considered and documented. This could be considered in the form of a value stream, to ensure that all activities are required in order to add value to the audit. The PDCA cycle could also be applied to review the plan.

Reducing waste

A lean audit is partly about helping to reduce waste – if it is conducted in a way that is wasteful it will lose creditability with auditees and stakeholders. Waste can be incurred at any stages of an audit, including:

- allocating inappropriate resource
- impact of disruption on the auditee
- failure to gather enough corroborative evidence, leading to misreporting
- inappropriate recommendations
- reporting on individual symptoms rather than the root causes of findings.

Where audits are repeated, this waste is also often repeated. *Table 7* shows some of the common types of audit wastage and their consequences. These can be reduced by steps including:

- proper planning
- ensuring the auditee and other stakeholders (including end customer) are consulted
- investigating the work performed previously on the area and then referencing this rather than repeating the same exercise
- full involvement of the customer throughout the process.

Table 7: Audit waste areas

Waste area	Common audit causes	Consequences
1. Defects	Failure to check audit findings with nominated business representative Unrealistic recommendations, for example cost more to implement than the benefit they create Defective planning, leading to the wrong areas or issues being reviewed	Mistakes in drafting reports cost time and effort to rectify and cause loss of confidence from the auditee
2. Overproduction	Excessive auditing of low risk areas Inappropriate timing of audits Management overload in responding to audit issues	Producing too many audits/audit findings, sooner or faster than is needed – when the audit resource used could have been better applied elsewhere
3. Waiting	Audits postponed or delayed due to staff shortages or time overruns on other projects	Audit has to stop because of resourcing/supply issues

Waste area	Common audit causes	Consequences
4. Not utilising talent	Not asking opinion or ideas from auditees

Not identifying members of audit team with previous experience of similar audits

Not using resources provided by lean and audit institutes and similar organisations | Not fully using the skills, talents and knowledge of staff and other business partners |
| 5. Transportation | Inadequate storage/referencing of working papers

Not using video conferencing or similar media rather than visiting all locations | Waste causing by having to move, or handle, components or work packages between stages |
| 6. Inventory excess | Inability to recover audit findings to enable efficient follow-up | Excessive storing of components or finished product |
| 7. Motion waste | Inadequate audit planning leading to too many repeat visits | Unnecessary physical movement |

Waste area	Common audit causes	Consequences
8. Excess processing	Too many review steps before report is issued or findings revealed so that action can be taken	Steps that are duplicated or otherwise unnecessary to achieve customer value

Creating flow of the audit and output by eliminating waste

There are two aspects of flow to consider for the audit:

1. The planning and organisation of the audit to ensure that it is conducted with minimum waste.
2. The forming of recommendations and reporting in a way that will ensure points are easily understood and accepted by the auditee.

I once arrived to conduct an annual audit I had conducted for the previous three years. I telephoned in advance to agree the details, but when I arrived at the location I found an empty field – the offices had been re-located (luckily only three miles away). On another audit I arrived on the agreed date to find that the client was not ready – I had the team on site but it was a week before they were able to provide some of the data we needed and had asked for. When conducting an audit of lean, it is even more important to ensure that proper planning has been conducted, including:

- Agreement of scope and objectives with key stakeholders.

- Risks being clearly identified – both for the subject of the review and the audit itself.
- Briefing information for the audit team (including site arrangements, culture and nature of the project and any sensitive issues).
- Informing auditees of timing of visit, ideally with interview schedulers and list of documents required.
- Agreeing logistic arrangements (including access to offices, parking, desk space, e-connectivity, etc.).
- Arrangements for agreeing factual accuracy and presenting findings (e.g. show and tell sessions).

Evidence to support findings is vital, to use an analogy:

> 'If the moment has come to tell people their baby is ugly, do yourself a favour and make sure you have the evidence to back it up.'
>
> Peter Voser: *What does a CFO expect from Internal Audit?*

The reporting of findings should also be aligned to lean. A 500-page report with over 50 recommendations is unlikely to provide what the auditee needs. Instead, the report should be concise and aligned with the lean objectives and approach of the organisation, in particular:

- Reduce waste verbiage – make the report easy to read and review.
- Provide clear recommendations, backed up by evidence.
- Provide positive as well as negative feedback so that best practice can be shared across the organisation.

- Be consistent with the organisation's ethos and lean approach – including stating benefits of any recommendations to the customer.
- Have clearly assigned and agreed actions – remember if the auditee has a better recommendation than yours that will meet all of the objectives, this is to be preferred, as it will ensure buy in and action.

Key tests for any lean audit recommendations should include:

- Will this add customer value or just waste?
- Have I reached the root cause of this issue?
- Have I considered all related implications?
- Can it be implemented effectively or is there a simpler way of achieving the same objective?

Responding to auditee (customer) pull

First we need to consider who the 'customer' of the audit is. This could include the auditee, other stakeholders, management and indeed the end customer. Most of them would probably prefer that the audit was not taking place – they see it as waste rather than adding any customer value. So the auditor needs to demonstrate the purpose and reason for the audit – and allow some flexibility so that the audit is not seen merely as an unwanted imposition. This may require time to explain the reasons and background for the review and to remove any pre-conceptions about the audit bad guys and gals. There may also need to be some flexibility to include additional areas important to the auditee, as long as these do not conflict with the overall objectives of the review. I found this an extremely useful approach, especially where auditees were willing to be quoted as the source of findings or suggestions in the report.

Reporting is one of the most contentious areas. Where the auditor needs to deliver bad news which could be detrimental to the auditee, it needs to be done on the basis of factual evidence based on metrics and data that are auditable (i.e. from stated sources, where the same finding and conclusion would be obtained by another auditor of similar competence). I remember one auditee who would always say that our team's draft report was full of 'factual inaccuracies'. Rather than argue with this assertion, I would work through the report with him, providing evidence to support the findings. I was also prepared to make changes to the tone and wording of the report where the underlying meaning remained – this usually made the report more acceptable to him and I normally got very good feedback at the end of the review, whilst not compromising the integrity of the report and its findings and recommendations.

One useful technique is to conduct a very short before and after review of the customers' expectations, including:

- Previous experiences and what could be done to improve this next time.
- Whether the audit is seen as adding management and customer value.
- Understanding the role of the auditors.
- Fit with the culture and expectations of the area under review.

- Technical competence and understanding of lean approach.
- Friendliness and approach of the team.
- Value in terms of:
  o Risk advice
  o Controls advice
  o Compliance advice
  o Added value.

Pursuing audit perfection

Perfection is certainly a goal that we should be aiming for from our audits. This will require constant learning and modification based on feedback from stakeholders and tweaking of the audit approach. For example, we need to avoid confirmation bias. We all have a preference to reports that confirm our own beliefs or preconceptions. If I write a report that praises management for their achievements, it will be well received by stakeholders and I will likely get good feedback. However, that does not make the work high quality – within a few months there could be a project failure due to risks that I have failed to report on. Without care the same bias can be applied to the whole of the audit process, impacting how we plan audits, conduct interviews and gather evidence. Hence perfection cannot be measured purely on the basis of feedback.

I once wrote a single recommendation about the need for a disaster recovery plan at a client. For this particular client there were a number of specific risks that made this a very high significance recommendation. They wrote a plan and the following year I reviewed it. I now had six recommendations relating to the disaster recovery plan! The client thought that this was unfair. But in pursuit of perfection I had to raise the new points.

Summary

By ensuring that we apply lean principles in the conduct of our own review, we will show empathy with the customer and the lean approach they are taking. This will enable a more effective audit – where in the spirit of lean it is seen as a collaboration rather than something to be feared.

An excellent source of further information on lean auditing is provided in the book of the same name by James C Paterson.

REFERENCES AND FURTHER READING

Chapter 1: Introduction to the History and Nature of Lean Projects

Lean Thinking: Banish Waste and Create Wealth in Your Corporation by James P Womack and Daniel T Jones

The Machine That Changed the World by James P Womack, Daniel T Jones and Daniel Roos

The Lean Startup: How Constant Innovation Creates Radically Successful Businesses by Eric Ries

Chapter 2: Lean Principles and Concepts

The Lean QuickStart Guide: The Simplified Beginner's Guide to Lean by Benjamin Sweeney, in partnership with ClydeBank Business (e-book)

Lean Change Management: Innovative Practices for Managing Organizational Change by Jason Little

Chapter 3: Identify and Specify Customer Value

Best Practices for Lean Development Governance (Three parts available from *www.ibm.com*) by Scott W Ambler

Waltzing with Bears: Managing Risk on Software Projects by Tom DeMarco and Timothy Lister, 2003, ISBN 9780932633606

Chapter 4: Identify and Map Value Stream

Learning to See: Value Stream Mapping to Add Value and Eliminate Muda (Lean Enterprise Institute) 1 December 1999 by Mike Rother (Author)

Application of Value Stream Mapping Tools For Process Improvement a Case Study in Foundry IOSR Journal of Mechanical and Civil Engineering (IOSR-JMCE) ISSN: 2278-1684, PP: 07-12 Mr Girish C Pude, Prof GR Naik, Dr PG Naik *http://iosrjournals.org/iosr-jmce/papers/ sicete(mech)-volume3/24.pdf*

Optimizing Software Development With Lean Value Chain Analysis by Vimal Mani, 2016, ISACA Journal

The Seven Value Stream Mapping Tools by Hines and Rich (see Peter Hines, Nick Rich, (1997 *International Journal of Operations & Production Management*, Vol. 17 Iss: 1))

Chapter 7: Pursue Perfection

Statik, – Kanban's hidden gem – talk by Mike Burrows *www.slideshare.net/asplake/statik-kanbans-hidden-gem*

Essential Kanban Condensed by David J Anderson and Andy Carmichael

Chapter 9: Governance of Lean Projects

What does a Chief Financial Officer Expect from Internal Audit? by Peter Voser, Chief Financial Officer, Royal Dutch Shell plc, 66th International Conference of the

Institute of Internal Auditors, Beurs van Berlage, Amsterdam 10 July 2007

Lean Auditing: Driving Added Value and Efficiency in Internal Audit by James C Paterson, Wiley, ISBN 9781118896884

INDEX

ITG RESOURCES

IT Governance Ltd sources, creates and delivers products and services to meet the real-world, evolving IT governance needs of today's organisations, directors, managers and practitioners.

The IT Governance website (*www.itgovernance.co.uk*) is the international one-stop-shop for corporate and IT governance information, advice, guidance, books, tools, training and consultancy. On the website you will find the following page related to the subject matter of this book:

www.itgovernance.co.uk/it_audit.aspx

Publishing Services

IT Governance Publishing (ITGP) is the world's leading IT-GRC publishing imprint that is wholly owned by IT Governance Ltd.

With books and tools covering all IT governance, risk and compliance frameworks, we are the publisher of choice for authors and distributors alike, producing unique and practical publications of the highest quality, in the latest formats available, which readers will find invaluable.

www.itgovernancepublishing.co.uk is the website dedicated to ITGP. Other titles published by ITGP that may be of interest include:

- Fundamentals of Information Risk Management Auditing
  www.itgovernance.co.uk/shop/product/fundamentals-of-information-risk-management-auditing

- Swanson on Internal Auditing
  www.itgovernance.co.uk/shop/product/swanson-on-internal-auditing-raising-the-bar

- Agile Governance and Audit
  www.itgovernance.co.uk/shop/product/agile-governance-and-audit

We also offer a range of off-the-shelf toolkits that give comprehensive, customisable documents to help users create the specific documentation they need to properly implement a management system or standard. Written by experienced practitioners and based on the latest best practice, ITGP toolkits can save months of work for organisations working towards compliance with a given standard.

Please visit *www.itgovernance.co.uk/shop/category/itgp-toolkits* to see our full range of toolkits.

Books and tools published by IT Governance Publishing (ITGP) are available from all business booksellers and the following websites:

www.itgovernance.eu   *www.itgovernanceusa.com*

www.itgovernance.asia   *www.itgovernancesa.co.za*

Training Services

The IT Governance training programme is built on the foundations of our extensive practical experience of designing and implementing management systems. Our training courses offer a structured learning path from Foundation to Advanced level for IT practitioners and lead implementers, and help to develop the skills needed to deliver best practice and compliance in an organisation.

Our classroom and online training programmes will help you develop the skills required to deliver best practice and compliance to your organisation. They will also enhance your career by providing you with industry standard certifications and increased peer recognition. Our range of courses offer a structured learning path in the key topics of information security, IT governance, business continuity and service management.

Full details of all IT Governance training courses can be found at *www.itgovernance.co.uk/training.aspx*.

Professional Services and Consultancy

IT Governance is a world leader in the field of IT GRC (governance, risk management and compliance) solutions. Our multi-sector and multi-standard knowledge and experience can accelerate your projects, wherever you are in the world. We're independent of vendors and certification bodies, and encourage our clients to select the best fit for their needs and objectives.

Our mission is to engage with business executives, senior managers and IT professionals, and to help them protect and secure their intellectual capital, comply with relevant regulations and thrive as they achieve strategic goals through better IT management.

We have a wide range of consultancy delivery methods, guaranteed to suit all budgets, timescales and preferred project approaches. To find out more, please visit *www.itgovernance.co.uk/consulting.aspx*.

Sign up to the Daily Sentinel

Want to stay up-to-date with the latest developments and resources in the IT GRC market? We will send you mobile-friendly emails with fresh news and features about your preferred areas of interest, as well as unmissable offers and free resources to help you successfully start your projects.

www.itgovernance.co.uk/daily-sentinel.